A LENTEN COOKBOOK

for Orthodox Christians

ST. NECTARIOS PRESS

Seattle, Washington

1982

1st Printing, November 1972
2nd Printing, April 1978
3rd Printing with revisions, September 1982
4th Printing, March 1987
5th Printing, June 1991

Library of Congress Catalog Card No. 72-79472
ISBN 0-903026-13-1

Be not forgetful to entertain strangers:
for thereby some have entertained angels
unawares.   Hebrews 13: 2

DEDICATION

IN HONOR AND MEMORY OF THE HOLY SEVEN
MACCABBEE YOUTHS AND BROTHERS AND THEIR
MOTHER SOLOMONE AND THEIR TEACHER ELEAZOR
WHO UNDERWENT MARTYRDOM THROUGH GREAT
TORMENTS SO AS NOT TO DISOBEY THE
MOSAIC FAST.

AND

TO ALL STRUGGLERS EVERYWHERE WHO TRY
TO KEEP THE HOLY FASTS OF THE CHURCH.

PREFACE

This cookbook has been the result of a dream of many of our parishioners to have an Orthodox Cookbook for the lenten periods of our church.

Many of our faithful are converts who have not grown up in an Orthodox environment where lentils, beans and seafood and other "fast-foods" were essential parts of their diets. Often to a new convert, especially a mother, the problem of "what do you eat?" assumes gigantic proportions during the Great Lent or on Wednesdays and Fridays.

To encourage and revitalize fasting within our Orthodox household, our parishioners have prepared this cookbook with the generous contributions of many throughout the world whose help and encouragement we gratefully acknowledge. We pray that along with your physical fast you also will begin to understand the importance of spiritual fasting.

May our Lord Who came into the world to defeat him "who holds sway in the world" and who gave us the weapons of "prayer and fasting" to overcome satan, strengthen us in our spiritual struggles.

St. Nectarios Orthodox Church

THE LIFE OF
OUR RIGHTEOUS FATHER AMONG THE SAINTS
EUPHROSYNUS THE COOK

(Commemorated September 11)

Our righteous Father Euphrosynus was born
of peasant parents and consequently was
reared without schooling. Later he entered
a certain monastery, was robed with the
holy Schema of a monk, and served the
fathers. But since he was of coarse coun-
try upbringing, he remained in the diffi-
cult obedience of serving in the kitchen,
being scorned and mocked by some of the
monks who had forgotten the purpose for
which they left the world. Yet the blessed
one endured this contempt with a most
courageous heart, wisdom, and tranquility
of mind, not being troubled in the least
by these things. Thus if he seemed illi-
terate according to his manner of speech,
yet he was not such in the true knowledge
which he possessed, as we shall see from
the following.

There was in that monastery at the same
time as the ever-memorable Euphrosynus a
certain pious priest who made fervent en-
treaty that it might be revealed to him
the good things which they that love God
shall enjoy. One night, therefore, while
the priest was asleep, it seemed as though
he were in a certain garden. With amaze-
ment and ecstasy he beheld most delightful
things. He also saw Euphrosynus the cook
of the monastery, who stood in the midst
of the garden and partook of the diverse
good things of that place. Having come
nearer, he inquired of the blessed one to

whom this garden belonged, and how he had
come to be there.

Euphrosynus replied, "This garden is the
abode of God's elect, and by the great good-
ness of my God I have my dwelling here."

Then the priest asked, "But what dost thou
do in this garden?"

He answered, "I have dominion over all the
things which thou dost see here, and I re-
joice and am filled with gladness at the
vision and noetic enjoyment of them."

Again the priest said, "Canst thou give me
something of these good things?"

"Yea, by the grace of my God, take from
whatever thou dost wish."

Then the priest pointed to some apples and
asked Euphrosynus if he might have of these.
Taking a portion of the apples, the Saint
put them in the priest's outer garment and
said, "Receive that which thou hast re-
quested and take delight therein."

At that moment the wood was sounded for the
fathers to arise for the midnight service.
The priest, having awakened and come to
himself, considered the vision to have been
a mere dream, but when he stretched forth
his hands to take his outer garment--O the
wonder!--he discovered in reality those
very apples which Euphrosynus had given him
in the vision, and he wondered at the mar-
velous fragrance which still remained with
them undiminished. Arising from his bed,
he placed the apples aside and hastened to

church. There he saw Euphrosynus. He
approached him and besought him with oaths
to reveal where he had been that night.

The blessed one replied, "Forgive me,
father, but I went nowhere at all this
night, but just now I have come to church
for the service."

The priest answered, "For this reason I
charged thee with oaths, that thou wouldst
be obliged to make manifest the great
works of God--and thou art not persuaded
to make known the truth?"

The humble-minded Euphrosynus then answered
the priest, "I was there where are found
the good things which they who love God
shall inherit and which thou hast sought
for many years to behold. There thou didst
see me partaking of the blessings of that
garden; for God, wishing to make known to
thy holiness the blessings of the Just,
hath wrought such a miracle through me,
the worthless one."

The priest said, "And what, Father Euphrosynus, didst thou give me from that garden?"

"Those delightful and most fragrant apples
which thou just recently placed upon thy
bed. But Father, forgive me, for I am a
worm and not a man."

At the end of matins, the priest related
to all the brethren his vision and showed
to them the apples from Paradise. The
brethren could sense their ineffable sweet
fragrance and felt great spiritual joy in
their hearts, and they marvelled at all

the priest narrated to them. And hurrying
to the kitchen to reverence the blessed
Euphrosynus, they found that lo, fleeing
the glory of men, he had already secretly
departed from the monastery and was not to
be found.

The brethren divided the apples among themselves and gave portions to many who visited
the monastery as a blessing, and especially
for healing, because whoever partook of
these apples was cured of their infirmities.
And thus many received benefit from the
gift of the holy Euphrosynus. They re-
corded the vision not only upon tablets,
but also in their hearts. And they strove
greatly to make themselves pleasing unto
God.

By the prayers of the righteous Euphrosynus,
may the Lord deem us also worthy of the man-
sions of Paradise. Amen.

Dismissal Hymn--Fourth Tone

Thou didst live righteously in great
humility, in labors of asceticism and in
guilelessness of soul, O righteous Euphrosynus. Hence, by a mystical vision, thou
didst demonstrate most wondrously the
heavenly joy which thou hadst found. Do
thou make us also worthy to be partakers
thereof by thine intercessions.

"But whosoever drinketh of the water that
I shall give him shall never thirst;"
(John 4: 14)

ON FASTING

The Holy Apostle commands us saying "Let
us put on the armor of light. Let us walk
becomingly as in the day; not in rioting
and drunkenness, not in chambering and
wantonness, not in strife and envying.
But put ye on the Lord Jesus Christ, and
make not provision for the flesh to fulfill the lusts thereof." From the time of
the Apostles, Prophets and Fathers till
our own day, it is evident from the life
of the Church that fasting is part of our
"armor of light"; it is a mighty weapon
against the enemy given into our hands by
the Saviour Himself, Who is a type and
example for us in all things and Who fasted
in the flesh in order to teach us to fast.
To those weak and ill, it is a medicine and
antidote--a bath in which to be washed and
cleansed. Armored with holy fasting, St.
Elias the Tishbite withstood Ahab and his
army singlehandedly and called down fire
from the heavens. By fasting St. Moses,
the seer of God and the **elders of Israel**
prepared to ascend the mountain in the
desert and behold the Glory of God. By
fasting the Three Children were shown forth
to be fairer than the other children in
Babylon in the house of the king, and
Daniel was shown forth to be a shepherd of
lions.

Fasting, therefore, should always be under-
stood as a thing most necessary in our
battle with the evil one. Only a man who
has lost his mind would put down his

weapons, strip himself naked of his armor
and then jump into the line of fire to do
battle with the enemy. Such a one would
be committing suicide. A man who calls
himself a Christian and does not fast, is
such a man. In the final analysis he who
does not fast does not believe in God, for
he does not really believe in the exis-
tence of the enemy and the great victory
gifted to us over him by our Saviour. He
who does not fast does not believe in Him
Who said to the enemy, "Man shall not live
by bread alone." This is why Apostolic
and Patristic canons proclaim that all who
do not keep the fasts have fallen away
from the Faith (i.e. have become excommu-
nicated), and our Holy Father St. Seraphim
of Sarov instructs us not even to speak
with such persons.

Those who fell away from our Holy Faith
through schism and heresy, by distorting
the dogmas and truth of Holy Orthodoxy, in
consequence distorted the life of the
Church also, and especially the teaching
concerning fasting. Thus, to the Latins,
fasting became primarily a means of atonement, satisfaction, retribution, payment
for sins committed or for earning merits,
wages, favor, etc. when all sins had been
payed for. The Protestants correctly ab-
hored the use of fasting as "works" which
won merits which, in turn, were banked as
surplus in the treasury of the Popes to be
dispensed to "poor souls" in purgatory;
the few that continued to fast, however,
were not able to free themselves from the
error of Anselm concerning atonement and
punishment. Thus, after some centuries of
keeping fasts as 'a pious and ancient cus-
tom', yet having lost the correct under-

standing and position of fasting in the
life of the Church, both Latins and Protestants have totally abandoned fasting.
Now we see that even those that were
nearer to Holy Orthodoxy in Liturgy and
practice--the Copts, Armenians, Jacobites,
etc.--in their last gathering in Addis
Ababa have "reformed" their rules concerning fasting. This was to be expected
since all have fallen into heresies and
are separated from the Holy Church. But
now we hear even from those who bear the
name Orthodox similar trends and aspira-
tions. For us sinful folk, who neverthe-
less are still Orthodox in our Faith, this
is one more indication that these people
are despisers and apostates from Orthodoxy.
They are only proclaiming to all that have
ears to hear that they no longer wish to
walk in the way and tradition of our
Saviour, the Apostles, Prophets, and
Fathers, but rather wish to make "provision for the flesh, to fulfill the lusts
thereof." Of them the Psalms say, "They
mingled with the nations (heathen) and
learned their works" and the Holy Apostle
says, "They have a form of godliness, but
deny the power thereof."

St. Abba Isaac the Syrian says, "The
Saviour began the work of our salvation
with fasting. In the same way, all those
who follow in the footsteps of the Saviour
build on this foundation the beginning of
their endeavour, since fasting is a weapon
established by God. Who will escape blame
if he neglects this? If the Lawgiver Himself fasts, how can any of those who have
to obey the law be exempt from fasting?
This is why the human race knew no victory
before fasting, and the devil was never

12

defeated by our nature as it is: but this
weapon has indeed deprived the devil of
strength from the outset. Our Lord was the
Leader and the first example of this victory, in order to place the first crown of
victory on the head of our nature. As
soon as the devil sees some one possessed
of this weapon, fear straightway falls on
this adversary and tormentor of ours, who
remembers and thinks of his defeat by the
Saviour in the wilderness; his strength is
at once destroyed and the sight of the
weapon given us by our Supreme Leader burns
him up. A man armed with the weapon of
fasting is always afire with zeal. He who
remains therein, keeps his mind steadfast
and ready to meet and repel all violent
passions."

Those who do not fast--especially those of
the clergy--teach that fasting consists in
not thinking and doing evil and quote from
our Saviour, the Apostles and Fathers to
support their views. They usually forget
that our Saviour, the Apostles and Fathers
all fasted the physical fast as well as
the spiritual fast. When man partakes of
the glory of God, he does not partake of
it in the spirit only, but physically also-
-in a complete sense. When one praises
God, he does not praise Him only in the
Spirit, but with physical voice also in
chant and prayer. When one worships God,
he does not worship him noetically only
but physically also--the body participat-
ing by standing in prayer, by making pros-
trations and using the fingers and hand
to seal itself with the sign of the Cross.
When one communicates God, he does not
communicate in spirit only but eats the

very Body and drinks the very Blood of
the Lord unto healing of soul and body.
Thus one praises God and is united with
God not in part, but completely as one
whole--soul and body. When one labors in
virtue, one labors not only noetically
but physically also, even unto blood, in
order not to deny our Saviour. Our Holy
Martyrs did not witness just by words and
thought, resisting evil in their hearts
and minds, but gave their bodies up to
torments and their heads to be cut off,
that they might remain with our Saviour.
Thus, since we are not just spirits, but
"wear flesh and live in the world," we
cannot possibly fast spiritually only and
not fast physically also. There is a
unity and interaction between the body
and the soul. They cannot be separated
while we are still in the body.

In the Ladder of Divine Ascent, St. John
writes "Satiety of food is the father of
fornication; an empty stomach is the
mother of purity." He who always keeps
his stomach full and he who fasts know
the strength of this saying.

Holy Transfiguration Monastery

SAINT EUPHRO SYNOS

THE COOK

TABLE OF CONTENTS

CLARIFICATION - - MARGARINE

Only margarines without milk or other
animal products should be used in these
recipes. Many "house brands" and diet
margarines are manufactured without
milk.

L I T U R G I C A L   O F F E R I N G S

PROSPHORON (ALTAR BREAD)

1 pkg. compressed or dry yeast
2 1/2 cups water
2 tsps. salt
6 3/4 to 7 cups flour

Dilute yeast in water. Add salt, then
half of flour and stir. Mix remainder
of flour with hand until dough is firm.
Knead until dough is smooth. Divide
dough and place in 8-, 9- or 10-inch cake
pans that have been floured only. Do not
grease pans. Keep in mind that dough
should be smoothed out to cover the bottom
half of the depth of pan. (See helpful
hints below). Take religious seal and dip
in flour, shaking off any excess flour
that may accumulate, and press seal firmly
in center of dough. Remove seal and let
dough rise until it is almost doubled in
bulk. Remember, dough will also rise in
oven and too much rising can erase seal
from dough. Take a toothpick and make
5 or 6 pricks around outer edge of seal
before baking. Bake in 400-degree oven
for approximately 30 minutes or until
done. Wrap in clean cloth while cooling
so crust will soften.

HELPFUL HINTS THAT SHOULD BE USED IN MAKING PROSPHORON

There are two methods that can be used
when placing and smoothing dough out in
cake pans:

   1. Divide dough for each Prosphoron
       in two portions and flatten the
       dough in two layers in the cake
       pan--one on top of the other.

A3

2.   After you have shaped the dough
     in the pan, wait until it has
     risen, then cut a line with a
     paring knife in a circular
     motion around outer edge of
     risen dough in pan.

ARTOKLASIA

2 pkgs. compressed or dry yeast
1/2 cup water
3/4 cup sugar
1 tsp. salt
1 1/2 cups water
1/4 cup oil (salad, corn, etc.)
5 1/2 to 6 cups all-purpose flour
1 tsp. cinnamon

Dilute yeast in 1/2 cup water. Add sugar,
salt and stir. Add water and oil.

Add 3 cups flour mixed with cinnamon and
stir until batter is smooth. Add remainder of flour until dough is soft but firm.
Knead until bubbles appear on surface of
dough and it is smooth and satiny in
appearance.

Divide dough into 5 equal parts and place
in 5-inch round pans. Let rise in pans
until almost double in bulk. Bake in
400-degree oven for approximately 15
minutes, or until tops are golden brown.
Remove from pans and cool on racks for
10 minutes. Brush tops lightly with
honey. When cool, sprinkle powdered sugar
on top.

KOLLIVA

1 cup wheat berries (hulled)
4 quarts water

Boil wheat berries until tender (approximately 2 hours, depending on type of wheat). Drain in colander, spread out on clean toweling (not terrycloth), cover with another towel and roll up to blot thoroughly. Depending upon how it is prepared, the wheat may be used immediately or spread out to dry further.

Ground walnuts or almonds, white or dark raisins (about 1 cup), chopped parsley, sesame seeds, pomegranate seeds, cinnamon (about 5 dashes), 1/4 tsp. cumin powder, etc., may be mixed into dry wheat before decorating.

DECORATING VARIATIONS:

1. Put mixed wheat into bowl and smooth the top. Cover with finely chopped walnuts. Make a slight indentation in the form of a cross and fill with raisins, pomegranate seeds, or other such fruit. The bowl may be decorated as desired. At serving time, add granulated sugar to taste (approximately 1/4 cup), mix well and serve.

2. Mound mixed dry wheat on plate or platter. Cover with a 1/4-inch layer of either finely ground walnuts or almonds, or flour which has been browned in a dry skillet. Sift confectioner's sugar over all, covering completely. Decorate with Jordan almonds, silver decors, etc., as desired. (continued next page)

KOLLIVA (continued)

DECORATING NOTES:

It is traditional to form a Cross on the
kolliva, and also to put a candle in it
for the Memorial Service. If using
small silver decors to make the Cross or
other formal decoration, one may cut the
desired shape out of adhesive tape
(white), lay it, sticky side up, on a
plate, and sprinkle the silver decors
on the tape to cover the tape form.
This may then be laid carefully over
the powdered sugar. It should be removed before serving. Jordan almonds
are also traditional.

In plain kolliva as prepared in decorating variation #1, honey may be used to
sweeten instead of, or in addition to,
sugar.

B R E A D S

BAKING HINTS FOR YEAST BREADS

1. All recipes using flour in this section have been measured using eastern, not western flours. That is, only flours such as Pillsbury and Gold Medal were used. If you use a western flour, you must measure a larger quantity than that called for in the recipe. Western flours have a tendency to require more flour to absorb a like amount of liquid. This is very important in keeping the bread recipes in balance.

2. Yeast--When using a compressed yeast, use only lukewarm water to dilute. When using dry yeast, use higher temperature water. Remember, using too hot water to dilute yeast can "kill" it. When in doubt, always use cool water.

3. Since you cannot use in lenten baking milk or eggs to brush on the surface of the bread or rolls, brush on water and sprinkle either with sesame or poppy seeds. The water wash will work in the same manner as an egg or milk wash, with the exception that the surface of the baked bread will not be shiny. However, the sesame or poppy seed will adhere to the surface. You will find this a very inexpensive but efficient method to glaze the top of the loaves.

B3

APPLE FRUIT LOAF

1 cup brown sugar, firmly packed
1/2 cup salad oil
2 tbsps. cooking sherry
1 tsp. vanilla
1 cup raisins
1 cup coarsely cut mixed candied fruit
1 cup chopped nuts
1 cup pitted fresh dates, chopped
1 1/2 cups coarsely shredded peeled
  raw apples
2 tsps. soda
2 cups all-purpose flour (sift before
  measuring)
1/2 tsp. salt
1 tsp. cinnamon
1/4 tsp. nutmeg

In large mixing bowl mix together brown
sugar, salad oil, cooking sherry and
vanilla. Stir in raisins, candied fruits,
nuts and dates. Stir in apples mixed
with the soda. Sift flour again into
mixture with salt, cinnamon, and nutmeg.
Stir to blend thoroughly.

Turn into greased and floured loaf pan
(5 x 9 inches). Bake in moderate oven,
350 degrees, for 1 hour 25 minutes or until toothpick inserted in center comes out
clean.

Allow loaf to cool in pan for about 3
minutes; turn onto wire rack to continue
cooling. Makes 1 loaf.

APPLESAUCE RAISIN BREAD

1 cup applesauce
1/4 cup melted margarine
1/2 cup granulated sugar
1/4 cup brown sugar, firmly packed
2 cups unsifted all-purpose flour
2 tsps. baking powder
3/4 tsp. salt
1/2 tsp. soda
1/2 tsp. cinnamon
1 tsp. nutmeg
1/2 cup seedless raisins
1 cup coarsely chopped pecans or walnuts

In a bowl combine the applesauce, melted margarine, granulated sugar and brown sugar, blending well. Stir in the flour, baking powder, salt, soda, cinnamon and nutmeg. Stir until smooth. Stir in the raisins and the chopped nuts. Turn batter into a well-greased 5 x 9-inch loaf pan or fluted mold with tube that holds about 1 quart. Bake in 350-degree oven 1 hour. Cool. This quick bread slices best the second day. Makes 1 large loaf.

ARAB BREAD

2 cups warm water
1 pkg. dry or compressed yeast
1 tsp. salt
5 2/3 cups unsifted flour (about)
1/2 cup yellow cornmeal
1/2 cup unsifted flour
Peanut oil or Corn oil

1. Measure warm water into large warm bowl.
Add yeast, stir until dissolved. Stir in
salt and 3 cups of the flour. Beat until
smooth. Stir in about 2 2/3 cups of flour
or enough additional flour to make a soft
dough.

2. Turn dough out onto lightly floured
board and knead until smooth and elastic,
about 10 minutes. Place in greased bowl,
turning to grease top. Cover; let rise
in warm place, until double in bulk,
about 45 minutes.

3. Punch dough down. Turn out onto
lightly floured board and form into a
ball. Place inverted bowl over ball of
dough and let rise at room temperature
for 30 minutes.

4. Meanwhile, mix together the cornmeal
and 1/2 cup flour. Divide dough into 6
equal pieces; shape each into a ball.
Dip each ball in peanut oil; then roll
in cornmeal mixture.

5. On a board lightly dusted with cornmeal mixture, roll each ball into an 8-
inch circle. Place on ungreased baking
sheets.

6. Bake at 450 degrees for 5 minutes.
Bread will puff up but will not brown as
it bakes. Lightly brown tops of loaves
by placing under hot broiler about
one-half minute.

APPLE COFFEE CAKE (FOUR-LAYERED)

1 recipe Basic Sweet Dough (page B8)
   (Makes two coffee cakes)
1 1/2 cups brown sugar, firmly packed
1 1/2 cups chopped nuts
1/3 cup flour
1 tbsp. cinnamon
Dash each nutmeg and cloves
1/3 cup melted margarine

For each coffee cake:
4 to 6 tbsps. softened margarine
4 to 5 tbsps. raisins or currants
1 medium-sized apple, peeled and chopped

Prepare a streusel mixture of the brown sugar, chopped nuts, flour, cinnamon, nutmeg, cloves and the 1/3 cup melted margarine. Roll out 1/2 of the sweet dough on a lightly floured board to a 16-inch square. Spread 1/2 of the square with 1 to 2 tbsps. softened margarine and sprinkle with 3/4 cup of the streusel mixture. Spread 2 to 3 tbsps. of the raisins or currants and about 3/4 of the chopped apple over the streusel. Fold the plain half of the dough over the filling.

Spread half of the rectangle with 1 to 2 tbsps. softened margarine and sprinkle with about 1/2 cup streusel, about 2 tbsps. raisins or currants, and the remaining chopped apple. Fold over dough to form an 8-inch square. Pinch edges of dough together to seal in filling. Place in a well-greased (use marg.) 8 or 9-inch square pan. Spread top with about 2 tbsps. margarine and sprinkle with 1/2 cup streusel. Let rise in a warm place until almost doubled in bulk. Bake in 350-degree oven for about 35 minutes. Repeat steps to make a second cake.

BASIC SWEET DOUGH

This sweet dough is soft--about as soft as you can handle without having it stick to your hands or the board for kneading. It does not require much kneading.

1/4 cup (1/8 lb.) margarine
1 tsp. salt
1/4 cup sugar
*1 cup Non-Dairy Cereal Blend (heat until just hot)
1 pkg. yeast, active dry or compressed
1/2 cup warm water
About 4 cups sifted all-purpose flour
Softened margarine

Place the margarine, salt and sugar in a large bowl; add the warm Cereal Blend, stirring to dissolve the sugar and salt and to melt the margarine. Soften the yeast in the warm water and add to the Cereal Blend mixture. Stir in 3 1/2 cups of the flour, 1 cup at a time, beating vigorously to blend. Scrape dough from the sides of the bowl and brush the top of the dough and sides with softened margarine. Cover dough and let rise in warm place about 2 hours, or until almost doubled in bulk. Then turn out on a well-floured board and knead lightly, adding flour until the dough is no longer sticky (do not use more than 1/4 to 1/2 cup flour on board). Shape and bake as suggested in recipes.

*CEREAL BLEND is a new highly poly-unsaturated non-dairy milk substitute found in the dairy section of the Safeway Food Stores. It can be purchased in pint or quart cartons and is an excellent milk substitute in baking.

BUBBLE RING

Balls of dough are layered in a tube pan
to make this unusual bread. The balls
break off into individual rolls for
serving.

1 recipe Basic Sweet Dough (page B8)
1/2 to 3/4 cups chopped nuts
About 1/2 cup (1/4 lb.) melted margarine

GLAZE:
1/3 cup dark corn syrup
2 tbsps. melted margarine
1/2 tsp. vanilla

Pinch off pieces of the Basic Sweet
Dough and with your fingertips shape
each piece into a smooth ball about 1
inch in diameter, tucking the edges under to make a smooth top. Place one
layer of balls, about 1/2 inch apart,
in a well-greased (use margarine) 10-
inch tube pan. Brush with about 1/3
of the melted margarine and sprinkle
with 1/3 of the chopped nuts. Arrange
two more layers, placing balls over the
spaces in the layer below, topping each
layer with melted margarine and nuts.
Let dough rise in a warm place until
almost doubled in bulk. Bake in 350-
degree oven for 35 to 40 minutes.

Make a glaze by mixing together the
corn syrup, 2 tbsps. melted margarine
and the vanilla. Pour glaze over the
bubble ring after it is baked. Let
the ring stand for about 10 minutes
before removing it from the pan.

GLAZED ORANGE ROLLS

1 recipe Basic Sweet Dough (page B8)
1/2 cup (1/4 lb.) softened margarine
1 cup sugar
Grated peel of 2 medium-sized oranges

ORANGE GLAZE--Simmer for 10 minutes:
1/2 cup sugar
1/4 cup light corn syrup
1/4 cup water
Grated peel of 1 orange
(Cool syrup slightly before glazing rolls)

Roll out Basic Sweet Dough to a rectangle
about 1/4 inch thick. Cream together the
margarine, 1 cup sugar and grated peel of
the 2 oranges. Spread mixture evenly over
the dough. Roll dough up as for a jelly
roll and chill. Cut chilled dough into 1-
inch slices and place in greased muffin
pans or 1 inch apart on greased baking
sheets. (Those baked on baking sheets
will be larger and flatter.) Allow rolls
to rise in a warm place until almost
doubled. Bake in 425-degree oven 10 to 14
minutes. While warm, top with glaze.

INSIDE-OUT CINNAMON ROLLS

Roll out 1 recipe Basic Sweet Dough (page
B8) to large rectangle, about 10 x 24
inches and 1/4-inch thick. Spread with 3
tbsps. soft margarine. Sprinkle with 3/4
cups brown sugar and 2 tsps. cinnamon.
Cut into strips 10 inches long and 1 inch
wide and roll separately into snail shape,
with sugar side out. Place rolls 1 inch
apart on greased baking sheet and let rise
until double. Bake in 350-degree oven for
20 to 25 minutes. These cinnamon rolls
have brown sugar mixture on outside.

BREAD STICKS

1 pkg. yeast, active dry or compressed
2/3 cup warm water (lukewarm for
    compressed yeast)
4 tbsps. salad oil
1 tsp. salt
1 tbsp. sugar
About 2 1/4 cups unsifted all-purpose
    flour
Poppy or Sesame seeds (optional)

1. Dissolve yeast in water; add salad
oil, salt, sugar and 1 cup of flour.
Beat until smooth.

2. Add enough remaining flour to make
a stiff dough. Turn out on floured
board and knead until smooth and elastic, using additional flour as needed.

3. Place dough in greased bowl, cover
with damp towel and let rise in warm
place until doubled in bulk (about 1
hour).

4. Punch dough down; divide in half.
Cut each half into 24 equal-sized
pieces; roll each, using palms of hands,
into 6 or 8-inch lengths. Place paral-
lel on greased baking sheets about 1/2
inch apart. Brush with water and
sprinkle with poppy or sesame seeds if
desired. Let rise in warm place until
almost doubled (about 30 minutes).

5. Bake in slow oven, 325 degrees, for
30 minutes or until golden. Makes 4
dozen.

CARROT BREAD

1 1/3 cups sugar
1 1/2 cups water
1 cup raisins (or candied fruit)
1 tbsp. margarine
2 large finely grated carrots
1 tsp. cloves
1 tsp. cinnamon
1 tsp. nutmeg

Bring the above ingredients to a boil,
then simmer for 5 minutes. Cover and
let sit for 12 hours or overnight.
Then add:

1 cup chopped walnuts
2 1/2 cups flour
1/2 tsp. salt
1 tsp. soda
2 tsps. baking powder

Bake in 2 loaf pans or 1 tube pan at
275 degrees for 2 hours.

NOTE: The carrots completely disappear;
this is a moist, delicious bread.

CINNAMON AND CARDAMOM ROLLS

Heat to simmering   1 1/2 cups unsalted
                            potato water

Mix together: 3/4 cup sugar
                         1 tsp. salt
                         1 tsp. orange peel
                         1/2 cup shortening
                         1/4 tsp. imitation
                            butter flavoring

Pour hot potato water mixture over this.

When lukewarm add and dissolve	2 pkgs. dry yeast

Add and beat well	1 cup sifted flour

Sift remaining flour with:	4 cups sifted flour 1 tsp. cardamom and 1 tsp. cinnamon

Add to above mixture.

Let rise in warm place until double.
Punch down and divide in three pieces.
Roll out 1/2-inch thick. Brush top with imitation butter and shortening mixture (melted).

Sprinkle filling on liberally and pat well.
Roll jelly-roll fashion and slice 1 inch thick.

Lay slices side up and close together in 9 x 13 pan (well-greased). Cover and let rise again. Bake at 400 degrees for 10 minutes or until brown. Yield: 2 dozen.

Frost while still warm. Be sure and reheat rolls to serve.

FILLING:

Melt	1/2 cup shortening 1/4 tsp. imitation butter flavoring

Mix together	3/4 cup brown sugar 3/4 cup white sugar 1 tbsp. cinnamon 1 cup raisins

FROSTING:

1 1/2 cups powdered sugar
2 tbsps. water
1 tbsp. shortening

CORN MEAL MOLASSES BREAD

Bring to boil in saucepan 1 1/2 cups water and 1 tsp. salt.

Stir in 1/3 cup yellow corn meal.

Return to boiling point, stirring constantly.

Pour into large mixing bowl.

Stir in 1/3 cup molasses and 1 1/2 tbsps. shortening.

Cool to lukewarm.

Dissolve 1 pkg. active dry yeast in 1/4 cup warm water.

Add to lukewarm corn meal mixture. Mix well.

Mix in half of 4 to 4 1/2 cups sifted all-purpose flour.

Add enough remaining flour to handle easily; mix with hand (dough will be sticky). Turn onto lightly floured board; knead, and let rise until double (1 1/2 hours).

Punch down, place dough in greased 9 x 5 x 3-inch loaf pan and pat into a loaf shape. Let rise until almost double (about 1 hour). Brush top with melted margarine, or water. Sprinkle with a little corn meal and salt. Bake until a rich brown in 375-degree oven for 40 to 45 minutes. Yields 1 loaf.

EASY NO-KNEAD BREAD

1 1/4 cups warm water
1 pkg. active dry yeast
2 tbsps. shortening
2 tsps. salt
2 tbsps. sugar
3 cups flour

Dissolve yeast in warm water. Add
shortening, salt, sugar and 1 1/2
cups flour. Beat with electric mixer
for 2 minutes. Add rest of flour all
at once and mix with wooden spoon or
rubber spatula. Mix 1 or 2 minutes.
Cover and let rise 30 minutes. Stir
down (about 25 strokes). Form into
loaf and put in greased loaf pan. Let
rise 40 minutes or until 1/4 inch from
top of pan. Bake at 375 degrees for
45 minutes. After removal from oven,
brush top with melted margarine if
desired.

ENGLISH MUFFINS

1 cup warm water
1 pkg. active dry yeast
1 tsp. sugar
2 tsps. salt
1/4 cup soft shortening
3 cups all-purpose flour

Dissolve yeast in water. Add sugar,
salt, shortening and flour. Mix until
well blended and dough is soft. Roll
out 1/4-inch thick on floured board.
Cut into 3-1/2-inch circles. Place on
corn meal-sprinkled baking sheet.
Sprinkle muffins with corn meal. Let
rise in warm place until double (1 hr.)
Bake on medium-hot ungreased griddle or
grill baker about 7 minutes on each
side. Makes 10 to 12 muffins.

FINNISH BREAD

1 1/2 cups hot water
2 tbsps. shortening
1 tbsp. sugar
2 tsps. salt
1 pkg. yeast, active dry or compressed
1/2 cup warm water
3 cups whole wheat or rye flour
2 1/2 cups unsifted all-purpose flour
  (or more)

1. Measure the 1 1/2 cups hot water into a large mixing bowl. Stir in shortening, sugar, and salt. Set aside to cool until lukewarm.
2. Meanwhile, dissolve yeast in the 1/2 cup warm water; leave about 5 minutes, then blend into the first mixture.
3. Stir in the whole wheat or rye flour; beat with a wooden spoon for about 1 minute. Add 2 cups all-purpose flour; blend.
4. Turn out on a floured (1/2 cup flour) board; knead for about 10 minutes (add more flour if necessary), or until surface is satiny.
5. Place dough in a greased bowl. Brush top with salad oil, and cover with a slightly damp cloth. Allow to rise in a warm place until nearly doubled, about 1 hr.
6. Punch down and knead lightly; divide dough in half. Shape each half into a round loaf, place on a lightly greased baking sheet, and press down with hands until dough is about 1-inch thick. Cover and let rise about 45 minutes or until nearly doubled.
7. Bake in a hot, 400-degree, oven for 25 to 30 minutes or until crust is light brown. Makes 2 loaves.

FRENCH BREAD

1 pkg. active dry or compressed yeast
1/4 cup water
1 cup boiling water
1 tbsp. shortening
2 tsps. salt
1 tbsp. sugar
About 6 cups sifted all-purpose flour

1. Use very warm water for dry yeast,
lukewarm water for compressed yeast.
Sprinkle dry yeast or crumble cake into
1/4 cup water. Let stand a few minutes,
then stir until dissolved.

2. Pour boiling water over shortening,
salt and sugar in large mixing bowl.
Add 3/4 cup cold water and cool to
lukewarm.

3. Add yeast and gradually beat in
enough flour to form a stiff dough.
Turn out on floured board and knead
until smooth and satiny.

4. Put in greased bowl; turn once,
cover and let rise until doubled, about
1 1/4 hours.

5. Shape into 2 oblong loaves about
14 inches long. Put on greased cookie
sheets. Let rise until doubled, about
1 hour. Brush with water and make 3
slashes across top with knife.
Sprinkle with sesame or poppy seeds
(optional).

6. Bake in 425-degree oven for 30
minutes. Reduce heat to 350 degrees
for 20 minutes more.

FRENCH ROLLS

1 pkg. dry yeast
1 1/4 cups warm water
1 1/2 tsps. salt
1 tbsp. soft shortening
3 1/4 to 3 3/4 cups sifted all-purpose
   flour
Sesame or poppy seeds

1. Measure warm water into a large
bowl. Add yeast. Let stand a few
minutes, then stir. Add half the flour,
the salt and shortening. Beat until
smooth.

2. Mix in more flour, a little at a
time, first with spoon, then with hand
until the sides of the bowl are clean.

3. Turn out dough on lightly floured
board. Knead dough until smooth and
little bubbles can be seen beneath the
surface.

4. Place ball of dough smooth side down
in lightly greased bowl, turning once to
grease the top. Cover and let rise in
warm place 1 to 1 1/2 hours.

5. Punch down dough by quickly pushing
the fist into center. Pull edges of
dough into the center. Turn over and let
rise again for 15 more minutes. Divide
dough into 12 parts. Form each into
buns. (To shape buns, pinch dough together into round form, then roll back
and forth gently on the cloth or between
hands to seal.)

6. With scissors, snip buns in half, then in quarters, cutting through almost to the bottom of buns. Brush with water and sprinkle with sesame or poppy seeds.

7. Let rise uncovered about 45 minutes (rolls should be double in size.)

8. Bake 20 to 25 minutes at 425 degrees or until tops are browned.

FRIED SQUAW BREAD

3 cups sifted all-purpose flour
1 tsp. salt
3 tsps. baking powder
1 tbsp. sugar
1 tbsp. melted margarine
1 1/2 cups water
Fat for deep frying
Confectioners sugar

Sift dry ingredients; add margarine and water. Mix thoroughly. Drop by tablespoon into hot fat, 375 degrees, on a frying thermometer. Cook for 2 to 4 minutes, or until brown. Drain on paper towels. Sprinkle with confectioners sugar. Makes 6 servings.

GINGERBREAD

1 1/2 cups flour
1/3 cup sugar
2 tsps. baking powder
1 tsp. ginger
1/4 tsp. salt
1/4 cup margarine
1/2 cup boiling water
1/2 cup molasses

Combine margarine and boiling water. When
the margarine melts, add the molasses.
Sift dry ingredients together. Stir
molasses mixture into the flour mixture
and beat just enough to make a smooth
batter. Spread in a greased 8 or 9-inch
square pan. Bake about 35 minutes at
325-degrees. Good served with walnut
sauce. (See sauce recipes).

HOMEMADE TWIN LOAVES

2 1/4 cups warm water
1 pkg. active dry yeast
6 to 7 cups sifted all-purpose flour
3 tbsps. sugar
1 tbsp. salt
2 tbsps. soft shortening

1. Add yeast to the warm water and let
stand 3 to 5 minutes. Stir.

2. Blend in about half the flour with the
sugar, salt and soft shortening. Beat
until smooth. Add more flour a little at
a time, first with spoon, then with hand
until the dough cleans the bowl.

3. Turn onto lightly floured board and
knead. Continue until the dough becomes
smooth and little bubbles appear beneath
the surface.

4. Place in greased bowl, turning once
to grease all sides. Cover and let rise,
in warm place, until double--about 1 hour.

5. Punch down dough by quickly pushing
a fist into the center. Turn over in
bowl. Cover and let rise 15 more minutes.

6. Turn out onto the board. Divide in two and shape into loaves.* Place in greased pans, 4 1/2 x 8 1/2 x 2 3/4 inches or 5 x 9 x 3 inches.

7. Cover and let rise in warm place about 45 minutes, or until almost doubled.

8. Bake 40 to 50 minutes in preheated 400-degree oven, or until well-browned on tops and sides. Remove from pans and cool on rack. Brush loaves with shortening for soft crusts.

*For easy shaping, make twin loaves. Divide dough into 4 equal parts. Round each into a ball. Put two in each pan.

HOT CASSEROLE BREAD

1 pkg. dry yeast or 1 cake compressed
1 cup water
4 cups sifted flour
1 tbsp. sugar
2 tsps. salt

1. Sprinkle dry yeast or crumble cake into water. Let stand for a few minutes, then stir until dissolved.

2. Combine flour, sugar and salt in bowl.

3. Add water and yeast, and mix. Add more water, 1/4 to 1/2 cup, to make a soft dough. Cover and let rise until doubled.

4. Beat down and divide dough between two round 1-quart heatproof glass casseroles that have been greased with shortening. Let rise until doubled; then bake in 400-degree oven for 40 minutes.

5. Remove from casseroles and brush crust with margarine.

INDIVIDUAL WHOLE-WHEAT BATTER LOAVES

1 pkg. dry yeast or 1 cake compressed
1 1/4 cups water
2 tbsps. honey, brown sugar or molasses
2 cups sifted all-purpose flour
1 cup whole-wheat flour
2 tsps. salt
2 tbsps. soft shortening

1. In large bowl of electric mixer, sprinkle dry yeast or crumble cake into water. Let stand for a few minutes; then stir until dissolved.

2. Add honey (or brown sugar/molasses), about half of each of the flours, the salt and shortening. Blend at low speed, then beat for 2 minutes at medium speed.

3. Stir in remaining flours with spoon. Cover and let rise until doubled, about 30 minutes. Stir down and spread evenly in 6 greased pans (4 3/4 x 2 5/8 x 1 1/2 inches). Smooth and shape tops of loaves with floured hands.

4. Let rise until batter reaches tops of pans, about 40 minutes. Bake in 375-degree oven for 30 minutes. Cool.

LAVASH (Flat Syrian Bread)

1 cup wheat flour
3 cups white flour
1 tsp. salt
2 cakes dry yeast (diluted in 1/2 cup
    warm water)
Add 1 tsp. sugar in yeast

Add enough luke warm water to above to form
stiff dough. Knead well. Let rise 3
hours to double. Punch down and let rise
for 1 hour more to double.

Roll out thin on floured board 1/8-inch
thick. Dough is somewhat sticky.
Sprinkle cookie sheet with a little
corn meal. Place the flat bread on
cookie sheet. Bake at 400 degrees for
about 3 to 5 minutes. Bread is soft
and light-colored. For a crisper dar-
ker bread, place bread under broiler
for a minute until it blisters and turns
brown (but bake the bread first).
Margarine on the top after cooking
gives a nice flavor.

LIMPA BREAD

1 pkg. dry yeast or 1 cake compressed
    dissolved in 1/4 cup water
1/4 cup firmly packed brown sugar
2 tsps. caraway seeds
2 tbsps. shortening
2 tsps. salt
4 cups sifted all-purpose flour
2 cups unsifted rye flour (about)

1. Sprinkle dry yeast or crumble cake into water in large mixing bowl. Let stand for a few minutes, then stir until dissolved.

2. In saucepan, mix 1/2 cup cold water, sugar, caraway, shortening, and salt. Bring to boil and simmer for 5 minutes.

3. Pour into large mixing bowl and add 1 cup cold water. Stir in 2 cups all-purpose flour. Add 1 1/2 cups rye flour and mix well.

4. Sprinkle 1/4 cup rye flour on pastry board and knead dough until smooth and satiny, using more rye flour as necessary.

5. Put in greased bowl, turn once, cover and let rise until doubled, about 1 1/2 hours. Punch down, divide, shape each half into a ball. Put on a greased cookie sheet. Make 3 cuts 1/2-inch deep in tops. Let rise until doubled.

6. Bake in preheated 400-degree oven for 35 minutes.

ONION BREAD

1 pkg. dry yeast or 1 cake compressed
1 cup water
2 tsps. sugar
2 tsps. salt
3 1/4 cups sifted all-purpose flour
   (about)
2 tbsps. melted margarine
1/2 cup coarsely chopped onions
2 tsps. paprika

1. Sprinkle dry yeast or crumble cake
into water, stir until dissolved.

2. Add sugar, 1 tsp. salt, and 2 cups
flour. Stir, then beat well.

3. Stir in 1/2 cup more flour, reserving 1/2 cup for kneading. Sprinkle
about 1/4 cup flour on pastry board.
Turn dough out on flour; knead until
smooth and satiny, adding remaining
flour if needed.

4. Put in greased bowl, turn once,
cover and let rise until doubled, about
1 hour. Punch down and divide. Pat each
half into a greased 9-inch round
layer cake pan or 8-inch square pan.
Brush with margarine and sprinkle with
onion. Punch onion down into dough so
surface looks dented. Let rise until
doubled, about 45 minutes.

5. Sprinkle each with 1/2 tsp. salt and
1 tsp. paprika. Bake in preheated 450-
degree oven for about 20 minutes. Cut
into wedges or strips and serve hot.

POORIS (Bread from India)

3 cups flour
1 cup whole wheat flour
1 tsp. salt
3 tbsps. melted margarine
Corn Oil for deep frying

Sift together the flours and salt. Add
melted margarine and rub into the flour
by hand. Gradually add enough water to
make a stiff dough. Cover with a damp
cloth and set aside for at least 1/2
hour. Roll the dough very thin, Cut
into 3-inch to 4-inch circles. Heat the
oil to 360-365 degrees. Quickly fry the
pooris, pressing down gently into the
oil with a perforated spoon or pancake
turner to make them puffy. When golden
on both sides and puffed, remove from
fat and drain on paper towels. Serve
very hot. Makes 18 3-inch pooris.

PUMPERNICKEL

1 1/2 cups cold water
3/4 cup yellow corn meal
1 1/2 cups boiling water
1 1/2 tsps. salt
2 tbsps. sugar
2 tbsps. shortening
1 tbsp. Caraway seeds
2 pkgs. dry yeast or 2 cakes compressed
1/4 cup water
2 cups mashed potatoes
4 cups rye flour
4 cups wheat flour

1. Stir cold water into corn meal in a
saucepan, add boiling water, and cook,
stirring constantly, until thick. Add
salt, sugar, shortening and Caraway
seeds and let stand until lukewarm.

2. Sprinkle dry yeast or crumble cakes
into water. Let stand a few minutes,
then stir until dissolved. Add yeast
and mashed potatoes to the corn meal;
mix well.

3. Stir in flours. Turn out on floured board and knead until smooth and satiny.

4. Put in greased bowl; turn once, cover and let rise until doubled.

5. Divide dough into 3 portions, form into balls, and let rest a few minutes. Roll each loaf twice as long and twice as wide as pan in which it is to be baked. Fold ends into center and over-lap slightly. Press sides to seal and then fold over in similar fashion to fit pan.

6. Put each one in a greased pan with seam side down. Let rise until doubled. Bake in preheated 375-degree oven for about 1 hour.

PUMPKIN BREAD

4 cups sugar
1 cup oil
4 cups pumpkin
5 cups flour
4 tsps. soda
1/2 tsp. cloves
1 tbsp. cinnamon
1 tbsp. salt
1 cup dates or raisins
2 cups nuts

Blend sugar and oil together. Add pumpkin, then dry ingredients. Mix in nuts and raisins.

Bake at 350 degrees for 1 hour.

Makes 3 loaves.

RAISIN-NUT BREAD

1 pkg. active dry or 1 cake compressed
   yeast
1/4 cup water (warm or lukewarm)
1/2 cup sugar
2 tsps. salt
1/4 cup shortening
2 cups hot water
6 1/2 to 7 cups sifted flour
1 cup seedless raisins
1 cup chopped walnuts

Soften dry yeast in warm water or the compressed yeast in lukewarm water. Add sugar,
salt, and shortening to hot water. Cool
to lukewarm.

Add 2 cups flour, stirring well. Add
softened yeast; mix well. Stir in
raisins and chopped nuts.

Add flour to make a moderately stiff
dough. Turn out on a lightly floured
surface and knead dough until smooth and
satiny (5 to 8 minutes).

Shape into a ball and place in lightly
greased bowl, turning once to grease
surface. Cover and let rise in a warm
place until double in bulk (about 1 1/2
to 2 hours). Punch down.

Divide the dough into 2 equal parts.
Shape each part into a smooth ball. Let
rest 10 minutes. Shape into loaves.
Place in 2 greased 9 1/2 x 5 1/4 x 2 3/4
inch loaf pans. Let rise until double.
Bake in 375-degree oven for 40 minutes.
When cool brush with confectioners icing
if desired.

CONFECTIONERS ICING: Beat together some
confectioners sugar, softened margarine,
and enough hot water to make it the
right spreading consistency.

ROUND BREAD OR ROLLS

2 cups warm water
2 pkgs. dry yeast
2 tsps. salt
2 tbsps. sugar
2 tbsps. soft shortening
5 1/4 to 5 3/4 cups sifted flour

1. Measure warm water into a large
bowl. Add yeast. Let stand a few
minutes, then stir. Add half the flour,
the salt and sugar. Beat until smooth.

2. Add the shortening, then more flour,
a little at a time. Mix in, first with
spoon and then with hand until the sides
of the bowl are cleaned.

3. Turn onto lightly floured board and
knead. Continue until dough becomes
smooth and bubbles appear beneath the
surface.

4. Place ball of dough smooth side
down in lightly greased bowl, turning
once to grease the top.

5. Cover and let rise in warm place
about 45 minutes.

6. Punch down dough. Turn over and
let rise again for 15 more minutes.
Divide dough into 2 or 4 parts for
loaves (or 10 to 12 parts for rolls.)

7. Round up each part into a ball.
Place balls on greased baking sheet or
in 8 or 9-inch layer pans. Flatten with
knuckles to 3/4-inch thickness. (The
rolls should be about 5 inches in
diameter; 2 loaves, 9 inches; 4 loaves
8 inches).

8. Slash tops of each round with a
sharp knife or razor blade to form a
diamond pattern. Let rise in warm place
20 to 30 minutes, or until doubled.

9. Bake 20 to 30 minutes in preheated
425-degree oven until well browned. Remove from pans to cool on racks.

TALAMEE
(Near Eastern Loaf Breads)

2 cups warm water
2 pkgs. active dry or 2 cakes compressed
   yeast
1/4 cup sugar
2 tsps. salt
2 tbsps. margarine, melted
1 tbsp. peanut oil or corn oil
5 1/2 cups unsifted flour (about)

Measure warm water into large warm bowl.
Add yeast; stir until dissolved. Stir
in sugar, salt, margarine, oil and 3
cups flour. Beat until smooth.

Mix in enough additional flour to make
stiff dough. Turn out onto lightly
floured board. Knead until smooth and
elastic, about 8 minutes.

Place in greased bowl, turning to grease
top. Cover; let rise in warm place until doubled in bulk, about 1 hour.
Punch down dough.

Turn out onto lightly floured board.
Divide into 4 pieces and shape each
piece into a smooth ball. Place on
greased baking sheets. Cover; let rise
in warm place 30 minutes. Flatten each
ball to about 1/2-inch thick. Let rise
about 45 minutes. Bake at 450 degrees
for 15 minutes.

WHEAT (CRACKED) BREAD

2 pkgs. active dry or compressed yeast
1/2 cup water, warm
3 1/2 cups water or potato water
1/4 cup firmly packed dark brown sugar
4 tsps. salt
1/4 cup margarine
6 to 7 cups unsifted all-purpose flour
5 cups cracked wheat

Sprinkle dry yeast or crumble cake into
water. Let stand for a few minutes; then
stir until dissolved. Pour hot water
over sugar, salt and margarine. Cool to
lukewarm. Add 3 cups flour and beat well.
Add cracked wheat and enough more flour
to make a stiff dough. Turn out on
floured board. Knead until smooth and
elastic, about 10 minutes. Put in
greased bowl. Turn once, cover, and let
rise until doubled in bulk. Punch down
lightly and again let rise until almost
doubled.

Put on floured board and divide into 4
equal parts. Cover, let rest 5 minutes.

Roll each piece into a 9-inch square.
Roll up as for a jelly roll. Seal the
ends of the roll and place each roll into a loaf pan (9 x 5 x 3 inches), making
sure ends of roll touch short ends of
pan. Let rise until double in bulk.
Bake in preheated 375-degree oven for
about 45 minutes.

WHITE BATTER BREAD

2 pkgs. dry yeast or 2 cakes compressed
2 3/4 cups water
6 1/2 cups sifted all-purpose flour
3 tbsps. sugar
3 tsps. salt
2 tbsps. soft shortening

1. In large bowl of electric mixer,
sprinkle dry yeast or crumble cakes
into water; let stand for a few minutes,
then stir until dissolved.

2. Add 3 1/4 cups flour, the sugar,
salt and shortening. Blend at low
speed; then beat for 2 minutes at
medium speed.

3. Beat in remaining flour by hand.
Cover and let rise until doubled, about
45 minutes. Stir batter, beating hard
for half minute.

4. Spread in two greased loaf pans (9 x
5 x 3 inches). Let rise until doubled
(about 20 minutes).

5. Bake in preheated 375-degree oven for
40 to 50 minutes.

D E S S E R T S

Cookies:

Pie Pastry:

Pies:

Turnovers:

COCONUT-CRUSTED APPLE DESSERT

6 large, tart apples, peeled, cored and
    sliced
1 cup brown sugar
1 1/2 tsps. ground cinnamon
1/2 tsp. ground mace
1/2 cup (about) all-purpose flour
1/4 cup fresh orange juice
1/4 cup margarine
1/2 cup flaked coconut

Heap apples in greased 8-inch round baking dish 2 inches deep. Mix 1/2 cup
brown sugar, spices, and 2 tablespoons
flour; sprinkle over apples. Pour orange
juice over all. For the topping, blend
1/2 cup brown sugar, the margarine, and
1/3 cup flour with a fork until crumbly.
Stir in coconut. Spread over apples.
Cover with foil. Bake in 425-degree
oven for 20 minutes. Remove foil; bake
about 15 minutes longer. Makes 6-8
servings.

MINI APPLE DUMPLINGS

4 cooking apples
Cinnamon sugar--1/4 cup sugar and 1 tsp.
    cinnamon
2 cups flour
2 tbsps. sugar
1 tsp. salt
2/3 cup shortening
5 to 6 tbsps. cold water
1/4 cup melted margarine
2/3 cup sugar
1 1/2 tsp. cinnamon
1/2 tsp. nutmeg
1 tsp. vanilla
1 cup water

C5

Peel, core and cut apples into quarters. Roll in cinnamon sugar.

For pastry, combine flour, 2 tablespoons sugar and salt. Cut in shortening until mixture resembles corn meal. Add 5 to 6 tablespoons water, a portion at a time, until dough forms ball.

Roll to rectangle, 1/8-inch thick. Cut in strips about 2 inches wide and 5 inches long. Wrap each strip around apple quarter. Place in baking dish, seam side down.

Top with melted margarine, 2/3 cup sugar and spices. Pour vanilla and water over dumplings.

Bake in 425-degree oven for 30 minutes or until golden brown, basting frequently with syrup from bottom of baking dish.

Yield: 16 mini-apple dumplings.

APPLE ROLL

2 cups sifted flour
1/2 tsp. baking powder
1/2 tsp. salt
1/2 cup tahini*
8 tbsps. water
3 or 4 apples, thinly sliced
1 cup brown sugar
1 cup raisins
1 tsp. grated orange rind
1 tbsp. cinnamon
2 tbsps. dry bread crumbs
2 tbsps. honey
1 cup chopped nuts

Stir tahini in jar until smooth. Pour
1/2 cup tahini in mixing bowl, and add
water slowly, a tablespoon at a time,
beating constantly until well-blended.

Add sifted flour, baking powder and salt;
knead until smooth and firm. (Add a few
more drops of water, if mixture is too
dry). Cover, let stand for 30 minutes.

With as little handling as possible,
divide dough in half. Roll out two
thin sheets and cover each with sliced
apples, raisins, nuts, orange rind,
cinnamon, bread crumbs and sugar. Pour
honey or 2 tablespoons orange marmalade
over fruit. Roll as in making jelly
roll. Dampen edges to seal.

Carefully place the two rolls on a
well-oiled baking pan, and with a sharp
knife, make gashes across top, about
1 1/2 inches apart.

Bake in 400-degree oven for 10 minutes,
then lower heat to 350 degrees and bake
for 20 to 25 minutes. Remove from pan
while still warm and sprinkle with
powdered sugar.

* Tahini is derived from ground sesame
seeds and has the consistency of peanut
butter.

DEEP DISH APPLE TAPIOCA

1/3 cup quick-cooking tapioca
1/8 tsp. salt
1/4 cup molasses
2 1/2 cups hot water
3 tart sliced peeled apples
1 cup raisins
1/2 cup sugar
1/8 tsp. each nutmeg and cinnamon
2 tbsps. margarine
Non-dairy Cool Whip topping

Mix tapioca, salt and molasses with water and cook, in a double boiler, 15 minutes.

Place apple slices in a greased baking dish (8 x 8 inches). Add raisins, sugar and spices. Dot with margarine.

Add tapioca mixture and bake in a 350-degree oven about 20 minutes or until apples are tender. Serve in small portions, hot or cold, topped with Cool Whip. Yield: 6 to 8 servings.

WAIKIKI BANANA BARS

1/4 cup shortening
1 cup brown sugar, firmly packed
1/2 tsp. vanilla
1/2 tsp. lemon extract
1 cup mashed, very ripe bananas
1 1/2 cups sifted flour
1 1/2 tsp. baking powder
1/2 tsp. salt
1/2 cup chopped nuts
1/3 cup powdered sugar
1 tsp. cinnamon

Combine shortening, sugar, flavorings, and banana in mixing bowl; beat hard. Sift flour with baking powder and salt; add to first mixture. Mix well. Stir in nuts. Bake in greased 11 x 7 inch pan at 350 degrees for 30 to 35 minutes. While warm, cut into bars. Gently roll in powdered sugar and cinnamon.

BLUEBERRY BETTY

6 tbsps. margarine
2 cups 1/2-inch white bread cubes
2 cups blueberries
4 tsps. fresh lemon juice
1/2 cup firmly packed dark brown sugar

Melt margarine and mix with bread. Put 1/3 of bread in baking dish, and top with 1 cup berries. Sprinkle with half the lemon juice and half the brown sugar. Repeat, ending with bread. Bake in 350-degree oven for 20 minutes.

APPLE CAKE

3-4 small apples peeled and diced
1 cup sugar
1 1/2 cups flour
1/2 tsp. salt
1 1/2 tsps. apple pie spice
1 cup pecans, walnuts or raisins
1 tsp. baking soda
1/2 cup salad oil
1 tsp. vanilla

Cover apples with sugar, let stand 20 minutes or until it makes a juice. Sift dry ingredients; add salad oil and nut-meats or raisins. Blend in apples. Pour into 8 x 10-inch greased baking dish and bake 50 minutes in 325-degree oven.

APPLESAUCE CAKE

1/2 cup shortening
1 cup light brown sugar (firmly packed)
1 cup canned applesauce
2 1/4 cups sifted flour
1/2 tsp. baking soda
1/2 tsp. salt
1 tsp. baking powder
3/4 tsp. apple pie spice (or 1/4 tsp.
    each cinnamon, nutmeg and allspice)
1 cup chopped nuts
1 cup raisins

Cream shortening, add sugar and beat.
Add applesauce. Sift together dry ingredients and add to mixture. Fold in
nuts. Bake in loaf pan or flat pan
lined with greased wax paper. Bake for
1 hour at 325 degrees. Cool 5 minutes,
then turn over on rack and peel paper.

LENTEN CHOCOLATE CAKE

3 cups flour
2 tsps. soda
6 tbsps. cocoa (Ghirardelli is excellent)
1 tsp. salt
2 cups sugar
3 tbsps. vinegar
2 tsps. vanilla
3/4 cup oil (salad, corn, etc.)
2 cups cold water

Measure flour, soda, cocoa, salt, and
sugar into large mixing bowl. Add vinegar, vanilla, oil and water and mix well.
Pour batter into greased 9 x 13-inch
baking pan. Bake at 350 degrees for 45
minutes. CHOCOLATE ICING: Mix powdered
sugar, cocoa, a little softened margarine. Add enough warm water to make
a smooth, creamy icing.

C10

CURRANT CAKE

1/2 cup oil
3 cups flour
1 tbsp. cinnamon
1/4 tsp. salt
1 cup currants or seedless raisins
1 1/2 cups sugar
4 tsps. baking powder
1/2 tsp. cloves
Juice of 2 oranges
Rind of 1 orange

Sift flour, baking powder, and salt together and place in deep bowl with sugar, spices and raisins. Add oil, orange juice and rind. Beat until thoroughly blended. Grease pan with oil and pour in batter. Sprinkle with sugar and cinnamon. Bake for 30 minutes at 350 degrees.

HONEY CAKE

2/3 cup honey
1/2 cup sugar
1 tsp. baking soda dissolved in 1 cup
    water
1/2 cup oil
1 cup walnuts, ground
1/2 cup walnuts, chopped
3 cups flour
2 tsps. cinnamon
1 tsp. nutmeg

Combine honey and sugar. Add water with baking soda, blend. Add oil, nuts (ground and chopped), cinnamon, nutmeg and flour. Mix well. Pour in greased and floured 9 x 9-inch pan. Let stand at room temperature for 1 hour before baking. Bake for 35 minutes at 350 degrees. Cut in square or diamond shapes.

RAISIN CAKE

In large saucepan boil 1 cup raisins
with 2 cups water for 10 minutes. Then
add 1/2 cup margarine and let cool.
In same saucepan put:
   1 3/4 cups flour
   1 tsp. soda
   1/2 tsp. salt
   1 cup brown sugar (firmly packed)
   1/2 tsp. cinnamon
   1/2 tsp. nutmeg
Bake in greased 10 x 10 pan in 350 degree
oven for 40 to 45 minutes.

TAHINI CAKE

3 cups flour
4 1/2 tsps. baking powder
1/2 tsp. salt
1/2 cup sugar
1 cup orange juice
1 cup tahini
1/2 cup raisins
1/2 cup chopped nuts

Add orange juice very slowly to tahini,
beating until well-blended.

Sift flour, baking powder, salt and
sugar together; add to orange juice mixture with raisins and chopped nuts. Mix
lightly and pour into cake pan which has
been brushed with oil and dust with flour.

Bake in 350-degree oven for about 1 hour.
Cool. Sprinkle with confectioners sugar
or cover with a warm, thin, syrup. (To
make syrup, boil 1 1/2 cups sugar and
3/4 cup water.)

CRACKER JACKS

1 cup granulated sugar
3 tbsps. white corn syrup
Pinch salt
1/2 tsp. soda
3 tbsps. margarine
Pinch alum

Cook ingredients to soft ball stage before adding soda. Pour over a gallon
of popped corn. For variety you may
use brown sugar.

STUFFED DATES OR PRUNES

Pit large dates or prunes. If the prunes
are very dry, put them in a strainer and
set over boiling water until they soften.
Cool before stuffing. Stuff with any of
the fillings listed below. Then roll in
granulated sugar or shake (4 to 6 at a
time) in a paper bag containing 1/4 cup
sugar. One teaspoon cinnamon may be
mixed with the sugar.

FILLINGS:

    Walnut or pecan meats, broken in
        pieces
    Salted almonds
    Brazil nut meats
    Candied ginger, cut fine
    Candied pineapple, cut fine
    Peanut butter mixed with orange juice

FRUIT BALLS

1 1/2 cups prunes, cooked and pitted
1 1/2 cups pitted dates
3/4 cup dried apricots
1/2 cup raisins
1 cup walnuts
1/4 cup sugar
1/4 cup concentrated orange juice,
   thawed
1 1/3 cup flaked coconut (3 1/2 oz. can)

Grind prunes, dates, apricots, raisins
and walnuts with coarse blade of a food
grinder. Add sugar and orange juice.
Form into 1-inch balls. Roll in
coconut. Makes 10 dozen.

FRUIT BARS

1 cup dried figs
1 cup pitted dates
2 cups walnut meats
Fine sugar

Put figs, dates and nuts through a food
chopper. Mix well. Press firmly into
a greased pan about 9 inches square.
Cut into squares or bars, or shape with
your fingers into balls. Roll in fine
sugar. Makes about 1 1/4 lbs.

VARIATION:

Use half walnut meats and half pecans.
Or add the grated rind of 1 orange and
1 tablespoon orange juice.

ORANGE COCONUT BRITTLE

2 1/4 cups granulated sugar
1/4 cup light corn syrup
1 tsp. shredded orange peel
1/2 cup orange juice
2 tbsps. margarine
1 1/3 cup flaked coconut (3 1/2 oz. can)

Grease sides of heavy 3-quart saucepan
with margarine. In it combine sugar,
corn syrup, peel, and orange juice.
Cook over medium heat to hard crack
stage (300 degrees), stirring occasionally. Remove from heat; stir in margarine. Pour in a thin layer in a
greased 15 1/2 x 10 1/2 x 1-inch pan or
large platter. Sprinkle coconut over it
evenly. When cold, crack. Makes about
1 1/4 pounds candy.

PEACH LEATHER

2 lbs. dried apricots
1 lb. dried peaches
Find sugar

Put dried apricots and peaches through
a meat chopper twice, using the finest
cutter. Sprinkle a board thickly with
fine sugar. Put the fruit mixture on it
and pat and roll it until it is 1/8-inch
thick. Cut in strips 1 1/4 x 2-inches.
Roll each strip in tight roll. Store in
tightly closed box.

PEANUT BRITTLE

2 cups granulated sugar
1 cup light corn syrup
1/2 cup water
1 cup margarine
2 cups raw or roasted peanuts
1 tsp. soda

Combine sugar, corn syrup and water in
a 3-quart saucepan. Cook and stir until
sugar dissolves. When syrup boils,
blend in margarine. Stir frequently
after mix reaches the syrup stage (230
degrees). Add nuts when temperature
reaches soft crack stage (280 degrees)
and stir constantly until the temperature reaches hard crack stage (305 degrees). Remove from heat. Quickly stir
in soda, mixing thoroughly. Pour onto
2 cookie sheets. As candy cools, stretch
it out thin. Loosen from pans as soon as
possible. Turn candy over and break it
in pieces.

PEANUT CEREAL CANDY

3 cups crisp rice cereal
1 cup salted peanuts
1/2 cup granulated sugar
1/2 cup light corn syrup
1/2 cup peanut butter
1/2 tsp. vanilla

Mix cereal and peanuts; set aside. Combine sugar and syrup. Cook, stirring
constantly until mix comes to a full
rolling boil. Remove from heat. Stir
in peanut butter and vanilla. Immediately pour syrup over cereal mix,
stirring gently to coat. Pat cereal
evenly into greased 8 x 8 x 2-inch pan.
Cool; cut in bars.

SUGARED POPCORN BALLS

2 cups sugar
2/3 cup light corn syrup
2/3 cup water
1/2 cup margarine
2 tsps. salt
1 1/2 tsps. vanilla extract
6 quarts popped corn

Mix sugar, corn syrup, water, margarine
and salt in saucepan; cook until mixture becomes brittle when tried in cold
water (270 degrees on a candy thermometer). Add vanilla and stir; pour slowly
over popped corn; mix. Grease fingers
with extra margarine and form into pop-
corn balls. Makes 24 medium balls.

SESAME CANDY

1 lb. sugar
4 oz. honey
1/2 cup water
1/2 lb. sesame seeds

Blend sugar and honey in pan. Add water
and cook over low heat, stirring frequently, for about 12 minutes, or until
mix reaches a soft ball temperature on
candy thermometer. Remove and add
sesame seeds. Spread on greased pan to
3/4-inch thickness. When cooled, cut
into 2 x 1-inch pieces.

TAFFY

4 cups granulated sugar
2 cups white corn syrup
1 cup water
2 tsps. glycerin
2 tbsps. margarine
1/2 tsp. cream of tartar

Mix and boil to crack stage (260 degrees). Add 2 tsps. vanilla. Pour into pizza pan and cool enough to pull. Pull until glossy and clear and form ropes on waxed paper, cutting into chunks when cooled.

WALNUT BONBONS

1/3 cup soft margarine
1/3 cup light corn syrup
1/2 tsp. salt
1 tsp. vanilla extract
4 1/2 cups sifted confectioners sugar
   (1 lb.)
Red and green food coloring
Walnut halves

Blend first 4 ingredients; mix in sugar and knead until blended. Divide mixture into halves and color one-half red and the other green. Shape mixtures into 1-inch balls and press a walnut half on each side of each ball. Store airtight. Makes 4 dozen.

CINNAMON TOAST DELUXE

1 lb. loaf fresh white bread
1 cup margarine
1 cup fine granulated sugar
1 tbsp. ground cinnamon

Cut slices of bread diagonally. Saute
half the slices slowly, 2 or 3 at a
time, adding margarine gradually until
each piece is golden brown on each side,
but not dark. Remove slices from skillet
and drop into a clean brown paper bag
containing a mixture of sugar and cinnamon. Shake gently and serve warm. To
pick up less sugar, put toast on a paper
towel to dry for a minute after browning.

NOTE: For variety, combine sugar and
cinnamon and add a little water to make
a paste. Dip bread into paste and saute
in margarine until browned. The sugar
and margarine caramelize and give the
toast a delicious crisp crust.

APPLESAUCE SQUARES

1 1/2 cups applesauce
1/4 cup brown sugar
2 tbsps. flour
1/4 tsp. grated lemon peel
1 tbsp. lemon juice
1/2 cup margarine
1/2 cup brown sugar
1/2 cup all-purpose flour
1/4 tsp. salt
1 cup quick-cooking rolled oats
1/2 cup flaked coconut
1/2 tsp. ground nutmeg

In small saucepan, combine applesauce,
the 1/4 cup brown sugar, the 2 tbsps.
flour, and the lemon peel and juice.
Cook and stir over medium heat until
thickened and bubbly. Cool. Cream
margarine and the 1/2 cup brown sugar.
Mix in the 1/2 cup flour and the salt;
stir in oats. Press one-half the oat
mix in an 8 x 8 x 2-inch pan. Spread
cooled filling over. Add coconut and
nutmeg to remaining oat mix; sprinkle
over filling. Bake in a 375-degree
oven for 30 to 35 minutes. Cool. Cut
in squares.

APRICOT SHORTBREAD

SHORTBREAD:
    1/3 cup soft margarine
    1/2 cup light brown sugar
    1 cup sifted flour

FILLING:
    3/4 cup dried apricots
    1 tsp. grated lemon peel
    2/3 cup sugar
    2 tsps. cornstarch
    1/3 cup chopped walnuts

Make shortbread in bowl with electric
mixer. Beat sugar and margarine until
light and fluffy. At low speed, beat
in flour.

Pat mixture evenly into bottom of 8 x 8 x
2-inch pan. Bake 12 minutes at 350 degrees. Cookie is light golden color.
Cool in pan on wire rack.

Now make filling as follows:

Place apricots in small saucepan. Add
just enough water to cover; bring to
boiling. Reduce heat and simmer,
covered, 15 minutes. Drain apricots,
reserving 3 tbsps. cooking liquid.

Chop apricots fine. Combine in small
saucepan with reserved liquid, lemon
peel, sugar, cornstarch. Bring to boiling, stirring; boil 1 minute.

Let filling cool 10 minutes. Spread
evenly over shortbread crust. Sprinkle
with walnuts. Bake 20 minutes at 350
degrees. Cool completely before cutting
into bars.

CINNAMON TEACAKES

1 cup soft margarine
1 1/2 cups confectioners sugar
2 1/4 cups flour
1 tsp. cinnamon
1/4 tsp. salt
1 tsp. vanilla extract

At medium speed, beat margarine until
light and fluffy. Then, at low speed,
blend in 1/2 cup sugar, the flour, 1/2
tsp. cinnamon, the salt, and vanilla
extract (dough will be rather stiff).
Chill 30 minutes or until stiff enough
to handle easily.

Roll dough into 1-inch balls. Place
balls 2 inches apart on greased cookie
sheets. Bake at 400 degrees for 9 to 10
minutes, or until delicately golden
brown. On a waxed paper, combine remaining sugar and cinnamon. Roll hot cookies
in this mixture. Cool.

COCONUT COOKIES

3/4 cup sifted flour
1/2 tsp. baking soda
1/2 tsp. salt
1/4 tsp. cinnamon
1/4 tsp. nutmeg
1/2 cup salad oil
1/4 cup water
1 cup brown sugar
1 tsp. vanilla
1 1/2 cups uncooked rolled oats
1 cup flaked coconut

Mix salad oil and water, sugar, vanilla, rolled oats, then flour mixture. Fold in coconut. Refrigerate 1 hour. Drop by teaspoonfuls on greased cookie sheet. Bake 10 to 12 minutes at 350 degrees.

VARIATION: For raisin cookies, substitute 1 cup raisins and add 1/2 cup chopped nuts if desired.

SPICY CURRANT BARS

1 cup brown sugar, firmly packed
1 1/4 cups water
1/3 cup shortening
2 cups currants
2 cups sifted flour
1 tsp. each of salt, baking soda and
    baking powder
2 tsps. cinnamon
1/2 tsp. nutmeg
1/4 tsp. cloves
1/2 cup chopped nuts

In large saucepan combine sugar, water,
shortening, and currants. Bring to a
boil and boil 3 minutes. Cool. Combine
dry ingredients and sift into cooled
mixture; blend well. Stir in nuts.
Spread evenly in greased and floured
9-inch square pan. Bake at 325 degrees
for 45 to 55 minutes. Cool; frost if
desired. Store in pan, tightly covered.
(Flavor improves upon standing). Makes
24 cake-like bars.

DATE-NUT COOKIES

1 cup brown sugar
1 tsp. vanilla
1 1/2 cups uncooked rolled oats
1/2 cup chopped nuts
1 cup chopped dates
3/4 cup sifted flour
1/2 tsp. baking soda
1/2 tsp. salt
1/4 tsp. cinnamon
1/4 tsp. nutmeg
1/2 cup salad oil
1/4 cup water

Mix salad oil and water, sugar, vanilla,
rolled oats, nuts, then flour mixture.
Fold in dates. Refrigerate 1 hour. Drop
by teaspoonsful on greased cookie sheet.
Bake 10 to 12 minutes at 350 degrees.

DATE PECAN BALLS

2 sticks margarine
1/4 cup granulated sugar
2 tsps. vanilla
2 cups flour
2 cups finely ground pecans
1 cup dates, diced (8 oz. pkg.)

Cream the margarine and sugar together.
Add vanilla and mix lightly. Add flour,
and again, mix lightly. Add pecans and
dates and mix until well-blended. Shape
mixture into balls, using 1 heaping teaspoon for each ball. Refrigerate for
1 to 2 hours. Place 1 inch apart on ungreased cookie sheet. Bake in 350-degree
oven for 20 minutes, or until lightly
browned. Remove from oven and roll at
once in confectioners sugar. Cool.
Sprinkle generously with confectioners
sugar.

FILBERT SPICE COOKIES

1 cup soft margarine
1 cup sugar
1/2 cup light molasses
3 1/2 cups sifted all-purpose flour
1 tbsp. ground ginger
2 tsps. ground cinnamon
2 tsps. cloves
1/2 tsp. baking soda
1/4 tsp. salt
1 cup chopped filberts

Cream margarine and sugar. Add remaining ingredients and mix well. Turn onto floured board and knead until smooth.
Shape into rolls 2 inches in diameter.
Wrap in wax paper and chill until firm.
Slice thin; bake on greased cookie
sheets in 350-degree oven for 8 to 10
minutes. Makes 6 dozen. Store airtight.

FILLED BAR COOKIES

First, prepare desired filling (see below) and cool.

FOR CRUST: (Mix thoroughly)
   3/4 cup soft shortening
   1 cup brown sugar
      Sift together and stir in...
         1/2 tsp. soda
         1 tsp. salt
      Stir in...
         1 1/2 cups rolled oats

Place one-half of this crumb mix in
greased 13 x 9-inch pan. Press and flatten with hands to cover bottom of pan.
Spread with cooled filling. Cover with
remaining crumb mix patting lightly.
Bake until lightly browned. While warm,
cut into bars and remove from pan. Bake
in 400-degree oven for 25-30 minutes.

DATE BARS: (follow recipe above)
Date Filling:
   Mix in saucepan...
      3 cups cut up dates
      1/4 cup sugar
      1 1/2 cups water
Cook over low heat, stirring constantly,
until thickened (about 10 minutes).

DATE-APRICOT BARS: (follow recipe above)
Date-Apricot Filling:
   Mix in saucepan...
      1 cup cut up dates
      2 cups mashed cooked dried
        apricots (drained)
      1/2 cup sugar
      2 tbsps. of the apricot juice
Cook over low heat, stirring constantly,
until thickened (about 5 minutes).

CRISPY FILLED COOKIES

1 3/4 cup sifted flour
1 tsp. baking powder
1/8 tsp. salt
1/2 cup soft shortening
1/2 cup brown sugar, packed
1/4 cup water
1 tsp. vanilla extract
1 cup crushed corn flakes

Mix shortening and sugar. Add flour, salt and baking powder alternately with water and vanilla. Mix in cereal. Refrigerate. Roll dough to 1/8-inch thickness. Cut with 3-inch round or scalloped cutter. Place on ungreased cookie sheet. Place rounded teaspoon of filling on each (recipe for fillings below). Top with another cookie. Press edges together with floured edges of fork. Bake for 10 minutes or until golden at 425 degrees.

PINEAPPLE FILLING:
    6 tbsps. granulated sugar
    4 1/2 tsps. cornstarch
    1 1/2 cups canned crushed pineapple
    1 tbsp. lemon juice (fresh or canned)

Mix ingredients and boil until the mixture thickens. Cool slightly and use as filling for cookies above.

RAISIN FILLING:
    1 1/2 cups raisins
    1/3 cup water
    1/2 cup sugar
    1 tbsp. cornstarch
    Pinch salt
    1 tbsp. lemon juice

(Cook same as above filling)

GINGIES (soft and puffy)

1/3 cup soft shortening
1 cup brown sugar
1 1/2 cups dark molasses
2/3 cup cold water
6 cups sifted flour
2 tsp. soda
1 tsp. salt
1 tsp. allspice
1 tsp. ginger
1 tsp. cloves
1 tsp. cinnamon

Mix shortening, brown sugar, and molasses thoroughly. Stir in cold water.

Sift together flour, soda, salt, allspice, ginger, cloves and cinnamon and stir in. Chill dough.

Roll out very thick (1/2 inch). Cut with 2 1/2-inch round cutter. Place far apart on lightly greased baking sheet.

Bake for about 15 minutes at 350 degrees, or when touched lightly with finger, no imprint remains.

GINGERBREAD BOYS

Follow recipe above--except mix in 1 more cup flour. Grease cardboard gingerbread boy pattern, place on the dough, and cut around it with a sharp knife. With a pancake turner, transfer cookie to greased baking sheet. Use raisins for eyes.

C27

CRISP HONEY COOKIES

1/2 cup margarine
1/2 cup honey
1 3/4 cup flour
1 tsp. soda
1/2 tsp. cinnamon
1/4 tsp. ground cloves
1/4 tsp. allspice
1/3 cup wheat germ

Cream margarine and honey. Sift together flour, soda, and spices and mix in wheat germ. Combine dry ingredients with creamed mixture. Chill about 1 hour. Roll on lightly floured board to about 1/8-inch thickness. Cut with floured cookie cutter. Put on greased cookie sheets. Bake at 350 degrees for 8 to 10 minutes. Cool. Spread thinly with frosting.

HONEY LEMON FROSTING:
   Mix 3/4 cup powdered sugar, 1 tbsp. honey and about 1 tbsp. lemon juice or enough to make frosting of thin spreading consistency.

JAM BARS

Cream together...
   1 cube margarine
   1/4 cup white sugar
   1/4 cup brown sugar
   1/2 tsp. vanilla
   1/2 tsp. lemon extract
Sift together and add...
   1 1/2 cups flour
   1 tbsp. baking powder
   1/2 tsp. cinnamon
   1/4 tsp. mace
   1/4 tsp. nutmeg

Mix well and spread half of mixture in a 8 or 9-inch greased square pan; press flat. Cover with layer of jam or marmalade. (If sweet jam is used, add juice of 1/2 lemon). Sprinkle remaining mixture on top. Add nuts if desired. Press lightly to smooth. Bake 25 minutes at 400 degrees.

JOE FROGGERS

4 cups flour
1 1/2 tsp. salt
1 1/2 tsp. ginger
1/2 tsp. cloves
1/2 tsp. nutmeg
1/4 tsp. allspice
1/3 cup water
1/2 tsp. rum flavoring
1 tsp. soda
1 cup dark molasses
1/2 cup shortening
1 cup granulated sugar

Sift together the flour, salt, ginger, cloves, nutmeg and allspice. Combine water and rum flavoring. Add soda to molasses. Cream shortening and sugar thoroughly. Add half the dry ingredients, half the water and rum flavoring, then half the molasses, blending well after each addition. Repeat. Chill dough for several hours or overnight.

On floured surface, roll 1/4-inch thick and cut with a 3-inch cutter. Bake on greased cookie sheet for 10-12 minutes at 375 degrees until lightly browned. Watch carefully so they do not burn. Let stand a few minutes; then remove. Makes about 3 dozen cookies.

MELOMACARONA

3 cups salad oil
1 cup orange juice
1 cup sugar
2 tsps. cinnamon
1/2 tsp. nutmeg
1 1/2 tsps. soda
7 cups flour
1 1/2 tsps. baking powder
1 cup chopped nuts

Blend oil, 1/2 cup orange juice, sugar
and spices. Mix baking soda and 1/2 cup
orange juice and add to the oil mixture.
(Hold over the mixing bowl as you do this
because it will foam over). Sift flour
and baking powder together and add to
make a soft-ball dough that can be
handled. Add nuts and blend. Shape into oblong cookies and bake at 350 degrees
for 30 minutes. Cool and dip into syrup.

SYRUP FOR MELOMACARONA:
    Boil 1 cup sugar, 1 cup honey and 1
    cup water. Dip cookie into the
    syrup while it is hot.

MOLASSES DROP COOKIES

1 cup soft shortening
1 cup brown sugar firmly packed
1 cup light molasses
1 cup boiling water
4 cups sifted all-purpose flour
1 tsp. salt
1 tsp. soda
2 tsps. baking powder
2 tsps. cinnamon
1 cup chopped nuts
1/2 cup wheat germ (optional)

Stir shortening and sugar together
until well-blended. Add molasses, then
boiling water.

Combine next 5 ingredients and sift into
sugar mixture; add nuts and wheat germ
if you wish to use it.

Stir until well mixed, making a very
soft dough. Chill until firm.

Drop by small spoonsful on lightly
greased baking sheet and bake at 400 degrees about 8 to 10 minutes or until
done. (Don't overbake). Makes about 7
dozen soft, puffy cookies.

NEW NORTHLAND COOKIES

Mix thoroughly...
    1/2 cup soft shortening
    1 cup brown sugar (packed)
Stir in...
    1/4 cup cold water
Sift together and stir in...
    1 3/4 cups sifted flour
    1 tsp. soda
    1/2 tsp. salt
    1/2 tsp. cinnamon
Mix in...
    1/2 cup cut-up blanched almonds

Mix thoroughly with hands. Shape into
a long smooth roll about 2 1/2-inches in
diameter. Wrap in waxed paper and chill
until stiff. With thin, sharp knife, cut
in thin slices 1/8 to 1/16-inch thick.
Bake on ungreased cookie sheet at 400 degrees for 6-8 minutes or until lightly
browned. Remove from pan immediately.

PEANUT BUTTER CHEWS

32 large marshmallows
2/3 cup peanut butter
4 tbsps. margarine
4 cups corn flakes
3/4 cup flaked coconut

Combine marshmallows, peanut butter and
margarine in top of double boiler; place
over simmering water. Heat, stirring
often, until marshmallows melt and mixture is creamy-smooth. Pour over cereal
and coconut in large bowl; toss lightly
until evenly coated. Drop by teaspoonsful on waxed paper. Let stand until firm.

PEANUT BUTTER COOKIES

Mix thoroughly...
    1/4 cup soft shortening
    1/4 cup margarine
    1/2 cup peanut butter
    1/2 cup sugar
    1/2 cup brown sugar (packed)
    1/4 cup *Cereal Blend

Sift together and stir in...
    1 1/4 cups all-purpose flour
    1/2 tsp. baking powder
    3/4 tsp. soda
    1/4 tsp. salt

Chill dough. Roll into balls size of
large walnuts. Place on lightly greased
baking sheet. Flatten with fork dipped
in flour. Bake 375 degrees for 10-12
minutes. *CEREAL BLEND is available at
Safeway Stores.

PINEAPPLE DROPS

Beat until light and fluffy...
    1 cup oil or margarine
    1 1/2 cups sugar

C32

Stir in...
    9 oz. can crushed pineapple with juice
Sift together and stir in...
    3 1/2 cups flour
    1/2 tsp. salt
    1 tsp. baking soda
    1/4 tsp. nutmeg
Stir in...
    1 cup shredded coconut

Chill dough for 1 hour. Drop by tsp. on
lightly greased baking sheet. Bake at
400 degrees 8 to 10 minutes.

PRINCESS DELIGHTS

1 cup shortening
1/4 cup margarine
1 cup sugar
1 cup brown sugar
1 tsp. salt
2 1/2 cups flour
2 tsps. baking powder
2 tsps. vanilla
1 cup coconut, shredded
Spiced powdered sugar (recipe below)

Cream shortening and margarine. Add
sugar gradually. Blend in sifted dry
ingredients. Add vanilla and coconut
and mix. Shape level teaspoon of dough
into balls. Bake on ungreased cookie
sheets at 325 degrees for 20-25 minutes.
Roll in mix of:

SPICED POWDERED SUGAR:
    1 cup powdered sugar
    1/4 tsp. nutmeg
    1/4 tsp. cinnamon
    Dash of white pepper

Mix all ingredients together and roll
cookies in mixture. Yield: 8 dozen.

RING AROUND THE COOKIES

1 cup soft shortening
1 cup sifted confectioners sugar
2 tsps. vanilla
1 1/4 cups sifted flour
1/2 tsp. salt
1 cup rolled oats

Mix shortening, sugar and vanilla. Add
flour, salt and oats and mix thoroughly.
Shape into 2 rolls 1 1/2-inches in diameter. Coat by rolling in either chopped
nuts or chopped candied fruit. Wrap in
waxed paper and chill until stiff (several
hours or overnight). Cut into 1/4-inch
slices. Bake on ungreased sheet at 375
degrees for 10-12 minutes.

TOM THUMB BARS

1/2 cup shortening
1/2 tsp. salt
1/2 cup brown sugar
1 cup flour

Combine shortening and salt. Add brown
sugar and blend. Add flour and blend.
Spread in greased 8 x 12 pan. Bake at
325 degrees for 15 minutes until lightly
browned. Remove from oven. Immediately
spread on topping:
    2 tbsps. flour
    1/2 tsp. baking powder
    1 1/2 cups shredded coconut
    1 cup nuts
    3/4 cup light corn syrup
    1 tsp. lemon juice
Blend and spread over hot bottom layer.
Bake another 25 minutes. Cool and cut
in rectangles.

HALVA WITH FARINA

2 cups sugar
4 cups water
1 cinnamon stick (optional)
Grated orange rind (optional)
1 cup oil
2 cups farina
1/2 cup almonds, blanched or 1/2 cup
    pine nuts browned in margarine

Boil sugar with water for a few minutes.
A cinnamon stick or orange rind may be
added for flavor. Combine oil and
farina in heavy saucepan. Cook, stirring constantly, until it comes to a
golden color. This must be done on very
low heat. Add blanched almonds or pine
nuts and continue cooking a few more
minutes. Add syrup and let stand for a
few minutes until it thickens. Pour into a greased form.

LEPPOLD SCHNITTEN

1/2 cup soft margarine
3/4 cup sugar (about)
1 cup unblanched almonds
1 cup sifted all-purpose flour
1 1/2 tsp. ground cinnamon
1/2 tsp. ground cloves

Cream margarine and 1/2 cup sugar until
fluffy. Put almonds through finest blade
of food chopper and add to mixture. Sift
flour, 1/2 tsp. cinnamon and cloves; stir
in. Pat into greased 13 x 9 x 2 inch pan.
Bake for 20-25 minutes at 350 degrees.
While hot sprinkle with mixture of 1 tsp.
cinnamon and 3 tbsps. sugar. Cut into
squares.

PEACH CRISP

1 cup unsifted all-purpose flour
1/2 cup granulated sugar
1/2 cup firmly packed brown sugar
1/4 tsp. ground nutmeg
1/4 tsp. salt
1/2 tsp. ground cinnamon
1/4 cup margarine
4 cups sliced fresh peaches
Grated rind and juice of 1/2 lemon
2 tbsps. water

Mix flour, sugars, nutmeg, salt and cinnamon. Mix in margarine with fork or fingers until coarse crumbs are formed. Put peaches in 9-inch shallow baking dish. Mix in lemon rind, juice, and water. Cover with crumb mixture; pat down so it sticks to fruit. Cover and bake in 350-degree oven for 15 minutes. Uncover and bake for about 30 minutes longer. Serve warm.

PEACH TAPIOCA

1/4 cup quick-cooking tapioca
Peach juice drained from canned peaches
  with enough water to make 2 cups
1/4 tsp. salt
1/2 cup sugar
2 tbsps. fresh lemon juice
2 cups drained sliced canned peaches
Non-dairy Cool Whip

Combine tapioca, peach juice, salt, and sugar in top part of double boiler. Cook, stirring frequently, until tapioca is clear. Blend in lemon juice and fold in drained peaches. Cook for 1 minute longer. Remove from heat. Top with Cool Whip, if desired.

HOT WATER PASTRY

1/2 cup shortening
1/4 cup boiling water
1 1/2 cups sifted pastry or cake flour
1/4 tsp. salt
1/4 tsp. baking powder

Put the shortening and boiling water in a
bowl. Stir until shortening melts. Add
the dry ingredients; stir with a knife
until well-blended. Put into a ball.
Wrap in wax paper and chill. Makes one
8-inch pie.

PLAIN PIE PASTRY

2 cups sifted flour
1 tsp. salt
2/3 cup shortening
6-7 tbsps. cold water

Sift together the flour and salt. Cut in
shortening with a pastry blender or with
your hands until mixed and crumbly.
Sprinkle water, a tablespoon at a time,
over the mixture and mix with a fork.
Gather up with fingers and form into a
ball. Let stand several minutes. Divide
dough in half and form two balls. Flatten
dough slightly and roll on lightly-floured
pastry board. Always roll from center out
to edge. Use light strokes. If edges
split, pinch together.

APPLE PIE

5-7 tart apples   1 tsp. cinnamon
3/4 cup sugar   1/4 tsp. nutmeg
2 tbsps. flour   2 tbsps. margarine
Dash salt
Pastry for 2-crust 9-inch pie

C37

Pare apples and slice thin. Mix sugar,
flour, salt, spices; add to apples. Fill
9-inch pastry lined pan. Dot with margarine. Cover with top crust. Bake in
400-degree oven for 50 minutes. If apples
aren't tart, add 1 tablespoon lemon juice
or grated lemon peel, if desired.

APPLE-RAISIN-NUT PIE

5 cups peeled and sliced cooking apples
1 cup raisins
1/2 cup chopped nuts
1 cup firmly packed dark brown sugar
2 tsps. ground cinnamon
Dash each ground cloves and nutmeg
Pastry for 9-inch lattice pie

Roll out half of pastry and line 9-inch
pie pan. Mix remaining ingredients and
fill lined pan. Roll out rest of pastry,
cut into 1/2-inch strips, and arrange on
top in lattice fashion. Moisten edges
with water and seal. Bake in 425-degree
oven for 10 minutes. Reduce heat to 375·
degrees and bake for 30-35 minutes.

APRICOT CRUMB PIE

2 tbsps. quick-cooking tapioca
3/4 cup granulated sugar
1/8 tsp. salt
2 lbs. fresh apricots, halved and pitted
Juice of 1/2 lemon
1/3 cup firmly packed light brown sugar
1/4 cup all-purpose flour
1/2 tsp. ground cinnamon
3 tbsps. margarine
Pastry for 1-crust 9-inch pie

C38

Mix tapioca, granulated sugar and salt.
Combine with apricots and lemon juice.
Pack into 9-inch pie pan lined with
pastry. Mix brown sugar, flour, and
cinnamon; cut in margarine to form crumbs.
Sprinkle over apricots. Bake at 425-de-
grees for 15 minutes; reduce heat to 375
degrees and bake for 30 to 35 minutes
longer or until apricots are tender.

BLUEBERRY PIE

2 1/2 cups fresh or frozen blueberries
1 cup sugar
1/4 cup flour
Dash salt
1 tbsp. lemon juice, fresh, frozen or
  canned
2 tbsps. margarine
Pastry for 2-crust 8-inch pie

Combine blueberries, sugar, flour, salt.
Fill 8-inch pastry lined pan. Sprinkle
with lemon juice. Dot with margarine and
cover with top crust. Bake in 400-degree
oven for 40-50 minutes.

CHERRY PIE

1 cup sugar
1/4 cup flour
1/4 tsp. cinnamon
1 can (1 lb. can) red sour pitted cherries
  (or 2 cups home-canned cherries with
   juice)
1/4 tsp. almond extract
1 1/3 tbsps. margarine
Pastry for 2-crust 9-inch pie

C39

In saucepan combine sugar, flour, cinnamon and undrained cherries. Cook over medium heat, stirring constantly, until mixture thickens and boils (about 7 min.). Remove from heat. Stir in extract. Pour into 9-inch pastry-lined pan. Dot with margarine. Cover with top crust; seal edges and crimp. Bake at 425 degrees for 30-35 minutes until nicely browned and juice bubbles through openings in crust.

Variation: If you prefer an uncooked filling, mix 2 tbsps. tapioca with sugar, cinnamon, undrained cherries, and extract. Pour into pastry-lined pan. Bake 5 min. longer.

Note: If home-canned cherries have been canned with a little sugar, adjust amount of sugar in recipe above.

CRANBERRY-APPLE PIE

1/2 cup sugar
2 tbsps. flour
1/4 tsp. cinnamon
1/4 tsp. salt
1 tsp. grated orange peel
1/2 cup honey
1 tbsp. margarine
3 cups fresh cranberries
2 cups diced, peeled apples
Pastry for 2-crust 9-inch pie

Combine sugar, flour, cinnamon, salt, orange peel, honey and margarine. Cook 2 minutes, stirring until sugar dissolves. Add cranberries and apples; boil 5 min. or until cranberries burst. Cool. Pour into pastry-lined 9-inch pie pan. Cover and bake at 425 degrees for 35-40 min.

WILD HUCKLEBERRY PIE

1 quart huckleberries
3 tbsps. quick-cooking tapioca
1 cup sugar
1/4 tsp. salt
Juice of lemon
1 tbsp. margarine
Pastry for 2-crust 9-inch pie

Stem and wash berries; drain. Mix with
tapioca, sugar and salt. Add lemon juice.
Roll out pastry. Use half to line pie
pan; trim edges. Pour in huckleberries.
Dot with margarine. Use remaining pastry
to cover pie. Moisten edges of pastry
and flute to seal. Cut vents in top.
Bake at 450 degrees for 10 min. Reduce
heat to 350 degrees and bake for 30-35
minutes longer. Sprinkle with additional
sugar if desired.

ORANGE-CRANBERRY-RAISIN PIE

1 1/2 cups sugar
1/4 cup fresh orange juice
1/4 tsp. salt
Water
3 cups cranberries
1 cup seeded raisins
1 tbsp. cornstarch
1 tsp. each grated orange and lemon rind
2 tbsps. margarine
Pastry for 2-crust 9-inch pie

Roll out slightly more than half of pastry
1/8-inch thick. Line pie pan. Bring
first 3 ingredients and 2 tbsps. water to
boil in saucepan, stirring constantly until sugar is dissolved. Add cranberries
and cook, stirring occasionally, until
berries pop open. Add raisins.

Blend cornstarch and 2 tablespoons water.
Add to berry mixture and cook until
thickened, stirring constantly. Remove
from heat and stir in fruit rinds and margarine. Pour into pastry-lined pan. Roll
out remaining pastry. Moisten edges of
filled pie with water and cover with top
crust which has been slit to allow steam
to escape. Press edges together with
tines of fork. Bake for about 25 minutes
in 425-degree oven.

Variation: For cranberry pie, follow
recipe above. Omit raisins and increase
cranberries to 3 1/2 cups.

PEACH AND APPLE PIE

3 cups sliced fresh peaches
3 cups sliced apples
3/4 cup sugar
2 tbsps. all-purpose flour
1/8 tsp. salt
1 tbsp. fresh lemon juice
1/2 tsp. grated lemon rind
1/4 tsp. ground nutmeg
1/2 tsp. ground cinnamon
1 tbsp. margarine
Pastry for 2-crust 9-inch pie

Mix sugar, flour, salt, lemon juice,
lemon rind, nutmeg and cinnamon. Line
pie pan with pastry. Half fill pan with
equal amounts of peaches and apples
(about 1 1/2 cups each). Sprinkle with
half of sugar mixture. Top with 3 more
cups of fruit and the remaining sugar
mixture. Dot with margarine. Adjust top
crust and bake in 425-degree oven for
40-50 minutes.

LATTICE-CRUST FRESH PEACH PIE

4 cups thinly sliced fresh peaches
3/4 cup sugar
3 tbsps. quick-cooking tapioca
1/4 tsp. salt
2 tbsps. margarine
Pastry for 2-crust 9-inch pie

Combine peaches, sugar, tapioca and salt.
Turn into a 9-inch pie plate lined with
pastry rolled 1/8-inch thick. Dot with
margarine. Roll remaining pastry into a
circle 1/8-inch thick. Cut into strips
1/2-inch wide. Arrange over pie in
lattice fashion. Trim, turn under and
flute edge. Bake in 425-degree oven for
40 minutes or until browned over the top.

RAISIN PIE

2 cups raisins (seedless)
2 cups boiling water
1/2 cup sugar
2 tbsps. flour
1/2 cup chopped nuts
2 tsps. grated lemon peel
2 tbsps. lemon juice
Pastry for 2-crust 9-inch pie

Cover raisins with boiling water, cook until tender (about 5 min.). Stir in
blended sugar and flour. Cook over low
heat, stirring constantly, until boiling.
Remove from heat. Stir in nuts, lemon
peel and juice. Pour into pastry-lined
9-inch pan, cover with top crust. Bake
at 425 degrees 30 to 40 minutes. Serve
slightly warm.

RHUBARB PIE

3 tbsps. all-purpose flour
1 to 1 1/4 cups sugar
1/4 tsp. salt
4 cups diced rhubarb
Grated rind of 1 orange
1/4 cup fresh orange juice
2 tbsps. margarine
Pastry for 9-inch lattice pie

Mix flour, sugar, salt and rhubarb. Add
orange rind and juice. Turn into pastry-
lined pie pan. Dot with margarine. Cover
with strips of pastry, lattice fashion.
Bake in 450-degree oven for 20 minutes.
Reduce heat to 350 degrees and bake for
about 20 minutes longer.

BAKED WHOLE PEARS WITH
RAISIN-NUT FILLING

4 large winter pears
1/2 cup sugar
1/4 cup each raisins and chopped nuts
1/4 tsp. each salt and ground mace
4 tsps. strained honey
1/2 cup hot water

Wash pears. Cut off stem ends and core.
Place in shallow baking dish. Combine
remaining ingredients except honey and
water. Fill pears with sugar mixture and
spoon remaining mixture around pears. Top
each pear with 1 teaspoon honey. Add water
to dish and cover. Bake in 375-degree
oven for 30 minutes. Uncover and bake for
10 minutes longer, or until pears are tender. Serve warm or chilled, topping pears
with sauce left in dish.

RAISIN BARS

1 cup sifted all-purpose flour
1/2 tsp. soda
1/2 tsp. salt
1 tsp. pumpkin pie spice
1/2 cup shortening, soft
1/2 cup firmly packed brown sugar
1/4 cup water
1 tsp. vanilla
1 cup quick or old fashioned oats,
  uncooked
1 cup raisins

Sift together first four dry ingredients
into bowl. Add shortening, sugar, water
and vanilla; beat until smooth, about 2
minutes. Blend in oats and raisins.
Spread batter evenly in greased 11 x 7-
inch pan. Bake 20-25 minutes at 350 degrees. Cut into bars.

SCOTCH PORRIDGE PUDDING

2 cups quick or old fashioned oats,
  uncooked
4 cups boiling water
1 tsp. salt
4 cups peeled apple slices (about 1/8-
  inch)
2 tbsps. margarine
1 cup firmly packed brown sugar
1/2 cup raisins
2 tsps. pumpkin pie spice

Heat oven to 350 degrees. Stir oats into
briskly boiling salted water. Cook 1 min.
for quick oats, stirring occasionally;
cook 5 minutes for old fashioned oats.
Cover pan; set aside. (The oatmeal may
be cooked ahead of time, covered and refrigerated until used.) (If cold oatmeal
is used, stir oatmeal before layering in
casserole and bake 30 to 35 minutes.)

Saute apples in margarine over medium heat
4 minutes, stirring occasionally. Add
sugar; cook over low heat, stirring until
sugar is dissolved. Remove from heat;
stir in raisins and pumpkin pie spice.
Starting with oatmeal and ending with the
fruit mixture, alternate layers of oatmeal
and fruit mixture in a greased 2-quart
baking dish or casserole. Bake uncovered
in 350-degree oven 20-25 minutes or until
edges bubble vigorously. Serve warm.

TEXAS AMBROSIA

4 navel oranges
2 red tart apples, peeled and sliced
Fresh lemon juice
3/4 cup chopped pecans
1 cup crushed pineapple
1 small coconut, peeled and shredded
3/4 cup cherries

Peel oranges, removing white membrane.
Cut oranges into sections, removing all
membranes. Sprinkle apples with lemon
juice to prevent darkening. Toss oranges
with apples, pecans, pineapple, coconut
and cherries. Chill and serve dusted with
confectioners' sugar, if desired. Makes
4 to 6 servings.

MARMALADE TURNOVERS

Roll standard pastry 1/8-inch thick and
cut into 4-inch circles. Put 1 tbsp. marmalade on one side of circle. Dot with
margarine and sprinkle lightly with cinnamon. Moisten edges. Fold over and press
edges together; seal with floured fork.
Bake for about 15 minutes at 425 degrees.

PUMPKIN RAISIN TURNOVERS

2 (10-oz.) pkgs. piecrust mix or use your
  own piecrust recipe
1 can solid-pack pumpkin (1 - 1 lb. can)
1/2 cup golden raisins
1/4 cup sugar
1/2 tsp. cinnamon
1/4 tsp. nutmeg
1/4 tsp. salt
1 tbsp. water
2 tbsps. sugar

Make up 2 pkgs. piecrust according to
directions, using 1/2 cup water. Roll
out on floured board to 1/8-inch thickness. Cut into eight 6-inch circles.
Make filling by blending in a saucepan
pumpkin, raisins, sugar, cinnamon, nutmeg and salt. Heat gently 3-4 minutes
for flavors to blend. Cool. Spoon 2 to
3 tbsps. filling in center of each pastry
circle. Dampen edges with water; fold
over and crimp. Brush each turnover with
a little water. Sprinkle each with a
little of the 2 tbsps. sugar. Bake 15 to
20 minutes or until pastry is light golden brown at about 400 degrees.

RAISIN-ORANGE TURNOVERS

1 3/4 cups seedless raisins
1 3/4 cups water
1/4 cup orange juice
1/3 cup brown sugar, firmly packed
1 tbsp. quick-cooking tapioca
1/2 tsp. ground cinnamon
1/4 tsp. salt
1 tbsp. vinegar
1 tbsp. margarine
2 tsps. grated orange rind
Standard pastry made with 2 cups flour

C47

Combine raisins, water and orange juice in
saucepan. Bring to a boil and boil for 5
minutes. Then add sugar, tapioca, cinnamon and salt. Cook, stirring constantly,
until mixture comes to a boil. Remove
from heat; add vinegar, margarine and
orange rind. Cool. Roll pastry very thin
(less than 1/8-inch) and cut into 6-inch
circles or 5-inch squares. Put about 3
tablespoons of filling on one side of
each circle or square, moisten edges,
fold over, and seal edges with a floured
fork. Bake for about 20 minutes at 425
degrees.

F I S H

BOUILLABAISSE

Put in a big kettle...
   1/2 cup olive or other oil
   1 carrot chopped
   2 onions chopped
   2 leeks cut small
   1 clove garlic (crushed)

Cook slowly until golden brown. Add...
   3 lbs. boned fish cut in 3-inch squares
   2 large tomatoes cut in pieces or
   1 cup canned tomatoes
   1 bay leaf
   2 cups fish stock, clam juice or water

Simmer 20 minutes. Add...
   1/2 cup shrimp, crab or lobster meat,
      cooked or canned
   1 dozen oysters, clams or mussels
   1/2 cup pimientos, cut small
   Few grains saffron

Simmer until the shells open (about 5 min.)

Season to taste with salt and pepper.

Add...
   Juice of 1 lemon
   1 cup dry white wine

Put in a soup tureen or bowl...
   8 slices french bread, toasted.

Pour the bouillabaisse over the bread.

Sprinkle with...
   1 tablespoon chopped parsley

Serves 8.

D3

BAKED COD, PIQUANT

1 1/2 lbs. fresh or thawed frozen cod
    fillets
1 tsp. salt
1/8 tsp. white pepper
1/4 cup melted margarine
Juice of 1 lemon
1 tsp. grated onion
Paprika
Minced parsley

Wipe fish with damp cloth or paper towel.
Cut into serving pieces and arrange in
greased shallow baking dish. Sprinkle
with salt and pepper. Combine margarine,
lemon juice, and onion and pour over fish.
Sprinkle with paprika. Bake in 325-degree
oven for about 30 minutes. Sprinkle with
parsley. Makes 4 servings.

NOTE: Also good with flounder, sole,
haddock, mackerel, halibut.

COD FILLETS IN TOMATO SAUCE

1 lb. package frozen cod or halibut
    fillets
1 clove garlic, minced
1 cup tomato sauce
1/4 tsp. pepper
1/2 cup dry, tart wine (optional)
1/3 cup oil
1 large onion, sliced
2 cups tomatoes
1 tsp. salt
1/2 tsp. marjoram

Heat oil in saucepan. Add garlic and
onion and cook until soft. Add remaining
ingredients except fish; cook 20 minutes
over moderate heat. Thaw and drain
fillets, add to tomato sauce, and cook 10
minutes. With spatula, remove fillets to
platter. If sauce has not thickened, cook
a while longer; then pour over fish. One
or two chopped potatoes may be cooked in
sauce before adding fish fillets.

COD WITH MUSHROOM AND WINE SAUCE

2 cans sliced mushrooms (3 ozs. each)
1/4 cup margarine
2 lbs. partially thawed frozen cod fillets
Salt and pepper
All-purpose flour
1/2 cup white wine

Drain mushrooms, reserving liquid. Cook
mushrooms in skillet in 2 tablespoons
margarine until brown; remove from
skillet. Cut fish into 8 pieces; roll in
seasoned flour and fry in skillet with
remaining margarine until brown on both
sides. Remove fish to heated platter.
Put mushrooms back in skillet; add mushroom liquid and wine. Heat; pour over fish.
Makes 4 to 6 servings.

BAKED FISH

3 or 4 lbs. Buffalo or Carp
Salt to taste
3 or 4 lbs. onions
1 No. 2 can tomatoes
1 tsp. chopped parsley
1/2 green pepper, chopped
3/4 cup oil

Wash and salt fish, leave whole or cut into pieces. Chop onions and add the tomatoes, chopped parsley, chopped pepper and
salt to taste. Mix well in a flat roaster
or baking dish. Lay fish on top. Pour
oil over all and bake at 350 degrees until
fish is very crisp and brown. (Fish may
be salted a few hours before cooking for
better flavor).
VARIATION: Add 1 cup rice to vegetables.

BROILED FISH FILLETS

2 lbs. fish fillets
1/2 cup olive or salad oil
1/4 cup lemon juice
1 tsp. mint leaves finely chopped
1/2 tsp. salt
1/4 tsp. pepper

Wash and dry fish fillets thoroughly.
Place on greased broiling pan. Brush
freely with mixture of oil, lemon juice,
mint leaves, salt and pepper. Broil
fish, basting occasionally with juice
from pan. Pour juice over fish when
serving.

GRILLED FISH WITH OIL AND LEMON SAUCE

2 lbs. fish

SAUCE:
1 cup oil
1 lemon (juice)
1 tbsp. parsley, chopped
1 tsp. mustard
1 tbsp. water
1 tsp. salt

Grill the fish; then beat all ingredients
and pour on grilled fish before serving.

FISH PIAKI

1 1/2 lbs. fish fillets
1 cup canned or 3 diced fresh tomatoes
1 bunch celery
2 small onions, chopped
1 clove garlic, minced
1/2 cup white wine
1/4 cup lemon juice
1/3 cup olive oil
Salt and pepper to taste
1/2 cup parsley
1/2 cup bread crumbs
Oregano
6 slices of lemon

Arrange fish fillets in a single layer in
greased casserole. Season fish with salt,
pepper and oregano. Make sauce by combining tomatoes, celery, onions, garlic,
wine, olive oil, lemon juice, salt and
pepper. Bring to boil and simmer until
vegetables are tender but firm. Pour sauce
over fish fillets. Sprinkle with parsley
and bread crumbs. Place lemon slices on
top. Bake in 350-degree oven for 30 to 40
minutes, or until done.

POACHED FISH, ITALIAN STYLE

2 tbsps. minced parsley
1 garlic clove, minced
3 tbsps. olive or salad oil
1 cup hot water
1 1/2 lbs. flounder fillets
1 tsp. salt
1/8 tsp. pepper
Pinch of dried oregano

Cook parsley and garlic in oil in skillet
for 3 minutes. Add hot water and bring
to boil. Add fish and seasonings. Cover,
bring again to boil, and cook for 5 to 10
minutes. Serve with the liquid. Makes
4 servings.

FISH ROE CAKES

1 jar tarama, 7 ozs. (Fish Roe)
1 onion, grated or 2 tbsps. chopped
  scallions
Salt and pepper to taste
5 potatoes, boiled
2 tbsps. cracker meal
Chopped parsley, mint or dill

Remove black membranes and scales from
tarama. Place in large bowl, and beat
to a thin paste. Mash potatoes thoroughly,
add to tarama, blending well. Shape into
patties, roll in flour or cracker crumbs,
and fry in vegetable oil until golden
brown.

FISH ROE DIP

1/3 of 8-oz. jar tarama
1 small onion, finely grated
Juice of 2 or 3 lemons
4 or 5 slices white bread
1 or 2 cups olive oil
Dash of garlic powder (optional)

Mash tarama and add grated onion. Add a
little olive oil and beat thoroughly until mixture resembles smooth paste. Remove crusts from bread, moisten, and
squeeze out excess water. Continue beating tarama mixture, and add alternately
small bits of moistened bread, olive oil,
and lemon juice. Beat until cream-colored.

SICILIAN FISH

4 slices of halibut or swordfish (or
   other thick fish, 1 3/4 to 2 lbs.)
1/4 cup olive oil
1 tbsp. chopped parsley
1 garlic clove, minced
1/2 cup white vinegar
2 lbs. tomatoes, peeled, seeded and
   chopped
Salt and pepper to taste
1 pkg. frozen peas, thawed (10 ozs.)

In skillet brown fish in hot oil. Add
parsley, garlic, and vinegar. Cook until liquid has almost evaporated. Add
tomatoes, salt and pepper. Simmer covered
for 5 minutes. Add peas; simmer covered
for about 30 minutes. Put fish on hot
platter and pour sauce over it. Makes 4
to 6 servings.

FISH SOUP

4 cups chopped onions
1/4 cup oil
2 lbs. tomatoes, peeled and chopped
Herb bouquet (parsley, bay leaf, marjoram)
1/2 cup white wine
1 chili pepper or 1 tbsp. chili powder
1/4 cup flour
6 cups water
Salt to taste
6 slices fish (4 or 5 ozs. each)
6 slices toast

Cook onions in oil until lightly browned,
add tomatoes, herb bouquet, wine and
chili and simmer until almost dry. Discard bouquet, add flour and water (or fish
stock made from bones;)and salt to taste.

Bring to a boil, turn low to simmer, add
fish, and cook until fish flakes easily
with a fork. Arrange toast in soup dishes
and carefully put a slice of fish on each
piece of toast. Divide soup among dishes
and serve. Makes 6 servings.

FISH STEW

3 or 4 large chopped onions
3 or 4 large sliced carrots
2 tbsps. chopped celery
2 tbsps. chopped parsley
1 minced green pepper
1 minced red pepper
3 tbsps. oil
2 glasses of water
2 lbs. boneless fish
Salt and pepper to taste
2 tomatoes or 1/2 can tomatoes
1 tsp. sugar
4 potatoes, quartered

Saute onions, carrots, celery, parsley,
green and red peppers in oil about 10
minutes. Add 2 glasses of water, salt,
pepper, tomatoes and sugar, and cook until tender. Add fish and boil for 15
minutes. Remove from heat and let stand
for about 2 hours, if possible. Add
potatoes which have been boiled. Reheat
stew and serve in the same casserole in
which it was made.

BROILED FLOUNDER

Flounder (2 to 3 lbs.)
1/4 cup lemon juice
Salt and pepper to taste
1/4 cup salad oil
1/2 tsp. prepared mustard

Clean fish, leaving on heads and tails.
Rub with salt inside and out and brush
with salad oil. Place on well-greased
broiler or shallow pan, and cut 3 or 4
gashes through skin. Cook under broiler
for 15 minutes or until fish flakes when
tried with fork. Turn and broil other
side until skin is brown and crisp. (If
fish is too large, do not turn). Remove
to large platter. Combine oil, lemon
juice, and mustard; beat with fork until
blended and thick. Pour over broiled
fish. Serve warm or cold.

BAKED FILLETS OF HADDOCK

1 lb. frozen fillets of haddock
3/4 cup white wine
1 small onion, thinly sliced, or 2
  green onions chopped
1/2 cup water
Oregano
5 tbsps. melted margarine
2 tbsps. lemon juice
1 small can sliced mushrooms
Salt
Pepper

Arrange onion slices in bottom of greased
shallow pan. Thaw fillets and drain well.
Rub each with salt and pepper, and arrange
over onions; brush over with melted margarine. Combine wine, lemon juice and
water, and pour around fish. Sprinkle
with oregano; cover with sliced mushrooms. Bake in 400-degree oven for about
20 minutes, basting with liquid in pan.

Arrange on hot platter for serving.

HALIBUT CREOLE

Place in baking pan...
    1 1/2 lbs. halibut in one slice
    Sprinkle with salt and pepper

Put over the fish...
    5 thick slices peeled tomato
    1/2 green pepper chopped
    2 tsps. chopped onion

Bake 25 minutes in 350-degree oven.
Baste 3 times during baking with the pan
juices and with 1/3 cup melted margarine.
Serves 4.

BARBECUED HALIBUT STEAKS

1 small onion, minced
1/2 green pepper, chopped
3 tbsps. margarine
1/2 cup chili sauce
1/2 cup catsup
Juice of 2 lemons
2 tbsps. brown sugar
1/2 cup water
1 tsp. powdered mustard
1 tbsp. Worcestershire sauce
1/2 tsp. salt
1/2 tsp. pepper
4 halibut steaks (2 lbs.)

Cook onion and green pepper in margarine
for 5 minutes. Add remaining ingredients
except fish and simmer for 10 minutes.
Broil halibut until done, brushing from
time to time with the sauce.

MACARONI WITH TARAMA

1/2 lb. thin macaroni
3 ozs. tarama
1 cup oil
1 cup finely chopped onion
2 quarts water
Tomato puree or fresh tomatoes
Salt to taste

Boil macaroni in salted water. Drain
without rinsing. Return to saucepan and
pour half the oil, which has been heated,
over the macaroni. Fry onion in the rest
of the oil until golden brown. Dilute
tomato puree, bring to boil and add a bay
leaf and seasoning. Add this to onion.
Cook until sauce thickens. Add tarama
after mashing it with a fork. Let it
boil with the tomato sauce for a few min.
Pour sauce over macaroni.

BROILED MACKEREL WITH POLITIKO SAUCE

1/2 to 3/4 cup olive oil
2 lemons, juiced
2 tbsps. ice water
1 onion, thinly sliced
1 cup parsley, chopped
Mackerel and lemon juice

Broil mackerel basting with lemon juice.
When cooked, place on platter and top
with sauce using ingredients above. Beat
olive oil and lemon juice until thick and
creamy. Beat in ice water. Stir in onion
and parsley and serve immediately.

Variation: Add a little oregano in place
of or along with the parsley.

D13

RUSSIAN MARINADE

2 carrots
1 green pepper
2 medium onions
Oil, pepper, salt
1/2 lb. fish without bone
Tomato sauce (or paste)

Salt fish and let stand. Stew vegetables
in a little oil. Cut fish into pieces,
turn in flour and fry separately in oil.
When vegetables are tender, add about 5
tablespoons of tomato sauce or paste and a
little bit of water. Add the fried fish
pieces to vegetables and simmer together
for 5 minutes. Serve cold with potatoes.

PAN SUPPER

1 pkg. frozen mixed vegetables
2 1/2 cups water
1 pkg. onion soup mix
1 tsp. salt
2 cups cooked lentils
1 can (7 ozs.) tuna chunks (drained)

In large frying pan with tight-fitting
lid, combine the first 4 ingredients,
stirring occasionally as they simmer 5
minutes. Add lentils and tuna. Cook
covered over low heat for 15 minutes.
Serves 6.

POTATO FISH STEW

3/4 cup olive oil
6 large onions, sliced
6 large peeled tomatoes or canned
  equivalent
1 bunch parsley, chopped
Salt and pepper
3 lbs. different small fish and shellfish (such as flounder, bass, perch,
  whiting, shrimps, clams, etc.)
6 medium potatoes, sliced
Toast

Pour oil into a casserole or Dutch oven
over low heat. When hot, add onions.
When these are soft, add tomatoes, parsley and salt and pepper. Let simmer for
about 15 minutes. Put in a layer of
sliced fish, boned and skinned if pre-
ferred, then potatoes and remaining fish.
When fish and potatoes are cooked through,
serve at once from the same casserole
over slices of toasted bread.

RED SNAPPER STEAKS WITH SHRIMPS

2 lbs. red snapper steaks
Salt and pepper to taste
4 tbsps. margarine
Few parsley sprigs, chopped
1 small carrot, minced
1 celery stalk, minced
1/4 tsp. dried basil
1 cup Rhine wine
1/4 lb. raw shrimps, shelled and
    cleaned
1 lemon, sliced

Wipe fish with a damp cloth and season on
both sides with salt and pepper. Melt 2
tablespoons of the margarine and use to
brush inside of a shallow baking dish.
Arrange fish in dish. Top with parsley,
carrot and celery. Sprinkle with basil
and add wine. Bake for 20 minutes at
350 degrees. Mince shrimps and saute in
remaining margarine for 3 minutes, or
until lightly browned, stirring constantly.
Pour over fish and bake for 10 minutes
longer, or until fish flakes easily with
a fork. Garnish with lemon slices.

BROILED SALMON

2 lbs. salmon, center cut, in one piece
Salt and pepper to taste
Juice of 2 lemons
1/4 cup olive oil
1 large onion, sliced

Wash and dry fish. Cut into slices 3
inches long and 1 inch wide. Sprinkle
with salt, pepper, lemon juice and olive
oil. Top with onion slices. Refrigerate,
covered, for 1 to 2 hours. Remove onion
slices. Broil fish for 5 to 8 minutes
on each side. Turn only one time.
Serves 4.

BROILED SALMON WITH HERBS

1 1/2 lbs. fresh or frozen salmon
  steaks, about 3/4-inch thick
1 tbsp. grated onion
Juice of 1 lemon
6 tbsps. melted margarine
1 tsp. salt
1/4 tsp. white pepper
1/2 tsp. crumbled dried marjoram
1 tbsp. minced watercress or chives
2 tbsps. minced parsley

Wipe fresh or thawed frozen fish with
damp cloth or paper towel; arrange on
greased broiler rack. Mix remaining
ingredients together and pour half over
steaks. Broil for about 6 minutes under
medium heat; turn and pour remaining
sauce over fish. Broil for 5 or 6 min.
longer, or until fish flakes easily
when tested with a fork. Remove to hot
platter; garnish with additional parsley. Makes 4 servings.

NOTE: Also good with swordfish, halibut,
striped bass, tuna, cod.

SALMON PATTIES

Combine canned salmon with cooked white
rice. Form into patties and fry in
vegetable oil.

SALMON STEAKS

6 salmon steaks (1-inch thick)
1/3 cup margarine
1/2 tsp. salt and 1/4 tsp. paprika
1 tsp. Worcestershire sauce
2 tbsps. grated onion

Place salmon steaks in shallow baking
pan. Melt margarine; add seasonings and
the Worcestershire sauce. Spread over
salmon. Sprinkle 1 teaspoon onion over
each steak. Bake in 425-degree oven
for 30 minutes.

SMELTS

Smelts
1/3 cup flour
1 1/2 tsp. salt
1/2 tsp. pepper

Wash smelts thoroughly and dry. Mix together flour, salt and pepper. Dredge
each fish in flour and fry in cooking oil
until golden brown. As they are fried,
place on platter and warm 1/4 cup vinegar
and pour over fried fish. One pound
serves 3. Serve with potatoes and a
salad.

NOTE: Lemon juice may be used in place of
vinegar.

FILLET OF SOLE IN ITALIAN SAUCE

2 small onions, chopped
1 clove garlic, minced
2 tbsps. oil
1 3 1/2-oz. can sliced mushrooms
1 small can tomato paste
1 8-oz. can tomato sauce
1 can water
1/4 cup chopped parsley
3 tbsps. lemon juice
1/4 cup white wine
1 1/2 tsps. salt
Pinch of pepper
1/2 tsp. dried rosemary
1 tsp. sugar
8 sole fillets (Red snapper may also be
  used)

Saute onion and garlic in oil until onions
are transparent. Add mushrooms, tomato
paste, tomato sauce, water, parsley, lemon
juice, wine and seasonings. Simmer about
30 minutes. Place 2 tablespoons of sauce
in the middle of each fillet. Roll up
like jelly rolls. Place in a shallow baking dish with the ends underneath to keep
them from unrolling. Pour remaining
sauce over the fish rolls. Bake in a 400-
degree oven for 25 minutes.
Yield: 8 servings.

FILLET OF SOLE IN WINE

1 lb. fillet of sole
1 4-oz. can mushrooms, sliced
1/2 lb. margarine
1 cup dry, white wine
2 green onions, chopped
Salt and pepper to taste

Season fillets; place over mushrooms and
chopped green onions in a saucepan.
Cover with wine and cook slowly until
fish is soft, about 10 minutes. Remove
fillets to heated platter. (Fish may be
browned slightly under broiler before
serving). Add margarine to wine and
mushrooms and boil down to half of ori-
ginal quantity, stirring constantly to
keep sauce very smooth. Pour over fish
in platter.

VEGETABLE STUFFED FISH ROLLS (SOLE)

2 medium carrots, shredded
2 parsley sprigs chopped
2 pimientos chopped
2 green onions chopped
2 cups stale white bread cubes
Melted margarine (about 1/3 cup)
Salt and pepper
2 lbs. fillet of sole

Mix together first 5 ingredients, 1/4 cup
melted margarine and salt and pepper to
taste. Spread each fillet with some of
the mixture. Roll fillets up from small
end and secure with toothpicks. Put in
a shallow baking dish and brush with
melted margarine; sprinkle with salt and
pepper. Bake at 375 degrees for 30
minutes or until done. Serves 6.

SPINACH STUFFED FISH FILLETS

2 medium onions, chopped
1 tbsp. margarine
2 lbs. frozen sole or flounder fillets
1 lb. fresh spinach or 1 pkg. frozen
spinach, cooked and drained (10 ozs.)
1 can meatless spaghetti sauce (15 1/2
ozs.)

Cook onions in margarine until tender but
not brown. Spread each thawed fillet with
cooked spinach and sprinkle with onion.
Roll up and put in shallow baking dish.
Pour on spaghetti sauce; bake for about
20 minutes at 350 degrees.

CURRIED TUNA

2 cups chopped onions
1 cup chopped apples
1/2 cup margarine
2 tbsps. curry powder
2 cups canned tomatoes
Salt
2 cans tuna (7 ozs. each)
Hot cooked rice
Chutney

Saute onions and apples in margarine until
wilted. Add curry powder and tomatoes;
cover and simmer for 30 minutes. Season
with salt to taste. Separate tuna into
flakes; add and heat. Serve with rice,
and chutney.

TUNA, PEAS AND RICE

1 small onion, minced
1/4 cup margarine
3 cups hot cooked peas and rice
1 or 2 cans tuna (7 ozs. each)
Salt and pepper to taste

Saute onion in the margarine until golden.
Toss lightly with remaining ingredients.
Serve hot. Makes 6 to 8 servings.

TUNA PIE

1 large onion, chopped
2 cups cooked rice
1 can tuna
Pastry dough

Use regular pie dough for top and bottom
and a rectangular pan for easier cutting
of pieces. Roll out dough to fit the
pan you have chosen. Saute onion and
add rice. Spread over bottom pie crust
and top with a can of tuna fish, spread
evenly. Put on top pie crust and bake
at 350 degrees for 30 minutes or until
crust is done.

POTATO-TUNA CASSEROLE

2 cups mashed potatoes
1 can tuna (7 ozs.)
1 tbsp. minced onion
1/2 tsp. curry powder
1/4 cup crushed potato chips

Mix all ingredients except potato chips
and put in shallow baking dish. Sprinkle
with potato chips. Bake in preheated
350-degree oven for about 30 minutes.

Makes 4 servings.

TUNA STUFFED PEPPERS

4 onions and/or leeks
3 sprigs celery
1 green pepper
1/2 carrot
1/4 cup rice
2 large cans tuna
Garlic salt to taste
Salt and pepper to taste
Green peppers

Mince onions and/or leeks, celery, green
pepper, carrot and parsley and brown
lightly in oil. Toss lightly into this
mixture the rice and tuna. Season with
garlic salt, salt and pepper. Fill
peppers. (Or cabbage leaves). Pour
sauce over peppers and bake at 350 degrees
for 1 hour.

SAUCE: Brown 2 tbsps. flour in 1/4 cup
oil. Season with paprika, salt, pepper.
Add 1 can tomato juice, stirring until
smooth.

SWEET-AND-SOUR TUNA

1 cup pineapple tidbits (7 ozs.)
1/2 cup vinegar
1/4 cup sugar
1 tbsp. soy sauce
2 tbsps. cornstarch
4 green onions, sliced diagonally
1 green pepper, sliced thin
2 tomatoes, peeled, seeded and cut
  into eighths
2 cans tuna (7 ozs. each)

Drain syrup from pineapple and combine it
with vinegar and sugar. Mix soy sauce
with cornstarch, and add. Cook, stirring
constantly, until clear and thickened.
Add onions, green pepper, pineapple and
tomatoes, and simmer for 4 minutes. Add
tuna, broken into large flakes, and cook
just long enough to heat. Serve with
chow-mein noodles if desired; or 1/4 cup
split almonds can be added to this dish.

WHITEFISH WITH PIQUANT SAUCE

1 lb. fresh or thawed frozen whitefish
  fillets
1 tbsp. cooking oil
1 tbsp. vinegar
2 tbsps. minced onion
1 tsp. salt
2 tsps. Worchestershire sauce
1/3 cup catsup
1/4 cup water
1 cup cooked green peas

Wipe fish. Cut into serving pieces.
Bring oil, vinegar, onion, salt, Worcestershire sauce, catsup and water to boil
in top part of double boiler. Add fish.
Cover and cook over boiling water for
about 25 minutes, or until fish is done,
stirring gently several times. Add peas,
heat thoroughly, and serve.
Serves 4.

NOTE: Also good with carp, mackerel,
weakfish, sea bass, pike, hake, cod.

WHITEFISH STEW

1 lb. fresh or thawed frozen whitefish
   fillets
1 tbsp. cooking oil
1 tbsp. cider vinegar
2 tbsps. minced onion
1 tsp. salt
2 tsps. Worcestershire sauce
1/2 cup catsup
1/4 cup water
1 tbsp. drained capers
1 cup cooked peas

Cut fish into serving pieces. Bring
onion, oil, vinegar, salt, Worcestershire,
catsup and water to boil in top part of
double boiler. Add capers and fish.
Cover, and cook over boiling water for
25 minutes, or until fish is done, stirring gently several times. Add peas,
heat and serve. Makes 3 to 4 servings.

M A I N   D I S H E S

Bean Plaki E3

Bean Soup E3

Beans, Baked, Vegetarian E4

Bortsch, Quick E4

Cabbage Rice E5

Cabbage Rolls E5

Chick Peas in Lemon Sauce E6

Chowder, Creole E7

Crab Sauce with Spaghetti E7

Clam Sauce with Spaghetti E8

Dolmathes E9

Green Peppers, Stuffed E10

Greens and Bean Curd, Oriental Style . E11

Hominy, Mexican E12

Leek Casserole E12

Lentil Fry E13

Lentil Soup E13

Lentil Soup with Tomatoes E13

Lentils, Baked E14

El

BEAN PLAKI

1/2 lb. navy beans or northern beans
1 clove garlic, minced
1 sprig celery, chopped fine
Pinch of sugar
Chopped parsley
1 chopped onion
3 tbsps. oil
1/2 cup tomato sauce
2 cups water
Salt and pepper to taste

Bring beans to boil in water, drain; add
fresh water and cook slowly until almost
done. Drain. Saute onion, celery, and
seasonings in oil for 5 minutes. Add
tomato sauce, water, beans and simmer 15
to 20 minutes until sauce and beans are
cooked. (Cooked chick peas may be prepared in this sauce in place of beans.)

BEAN SOUP

1 lb. great northern beans
1 cup diced onions
1 cup diced celery
1 cup diced carrots
1/2 cup diced green pepper
2 tbsps. parsley leaves
2 tbsps. olive or vegetable oil
2 cups tomatoes
1 tbsp. flour
1 onion, cut fine
Tarragon

E3

Wash beans and put to boil in cool water
for 10 minutes. In another pan, boil 2
quarts water. Strain beans, add new boiling water, all vegetables and boil until
beans are done--about two hours. In frying pan put oil and flour and fry until
deep brown. Add onion, cut fine, and fry
10 minutes. Add tomatoes and boil 10 to
15 minutes, mixing constantly. Add
tarragon. Strain mixture into soup and
mix well. If not sour enough, add a
little vinegar to taste.

VEGETARIAN BAKED BEANS

Saute until yellow in 2 tablespoons
margarine...
    1/3 cup minced onion

Stir in...
    16 oz. can vegetarian baked beans
    2 tbsps. dark molasses
    1/4 cup catsup

Pour into 1 quart baking dish.
Bake at 350 degrees for 25 minutes.

QUICK BORTSCH

Use a dehydrated vegetable broth (from a
health food store or in some markets).
Make the broth as directed on package,
grate canned beets (1/3 to 1/2 cup for
each serving), add liquid from canned
beets as part of total liquid. Add a
dash of catsup and serve with lemon
juice or vinegar to taste.

CABBAGE RICE

3 cups chopped cabbage
3 tbsps. tomato paste
1/4 cup olive or other oil
1 1/2 tsp. salt
1 cup long-grain rice
2 cups water
2 tsps. chopped parsley
1/4 tsp. pepper

Cook chopped cabbage and seasonings in
oil over low heat for 20 minutes. Add
water and tomato paste; bring to a boil.
Add rice; reduce heat, cover and simmer
until rice is light and fluffy.

CABBAGE ROLLS

1 large head cabbage
1 tsp. salt
2 cloves garlic, chopped
Juice of 3 lemons
Stuffing (recipe below)

Carve out thick core from center of cabbage. Drop cabbage into salted, boiling
water, core end down. Boil a few minutes
until leaves are softened. While boiling,
loosen each leaf with a long fork, remove
and place in a dish to cool. Remove
heavy center stems from the leaves. If
the leaves are extremely large, cut in
half. Fill each leaf with 1 teaspoon of
stuffing and roll into the shape of a
cigar. Place cabbage rolls in casserole,
alternating the direction of each layer.
Add the salt and garlic. Press with inverted dish and leave dish in place
throughout the cooking time. Add enough
water to cover. Cover casserole and cook
over medium heat for 45 minutes. Add
lemon and cook 10 minutes more.

STUFFING:

1/2 cup chick peas
1 tsp. oil
1 cup rice or cracked wheat
1/2 bunch parsley, minced
Salt and pepper, to taste
Pinch cinnamon, nutmeg and allspice

Soak chick peas overnight. The following
day, drain and rub peas with fingers to
remove outer skins. Mix peas with oil,
rice, parsley, salt, pepper and spices.

CHICK PEAS IN LEMON SAUCE

1 can cooked chick peas or garbanzo beans
1 tsp. salt
2 cups water
Juice of 1 lemon
1/2 cup chopped onions
4 tbsps. olive or vegetable oil
Pepper
1 tbsp. flour

Cook chopped onions in oil until soft.
(Do not brown). Add salt, pepper, water,
and boil for 15 minutes over moderate
heat. Add drained chick peas and cook
5 minutes. In small bowl, add lemon
juice from a half or whole lemon, according to taste. With a fork, stir in flour
and beat until thick and smooth. Gradually add small amount of hot liquid
from pot, beating constantly to blend.
Combine this lemon mixture with chick
peas, and stir over low heat until
slightly thickened.

E6

CREOLE CHOWDER

Mince the following ingredients and
saute in 1/4 cup oil:

1 large onion	2 sprigs celery
1 clove garlic	1 green pepper
2 leeks	

Add 2 quarts hot water, 1 small can
stewed tomatoes, 1 bay leaf, desired
seasonings, and the following additional
diced vegetables:

1 onion	1 kohlrabi
4 sprigs celery	1 green pepper
1 carrot	1 turnip
1 potato	Parsley

Add 1/2 cup rice and simmer gently for
30 minutes. For thickening, brown 3
tablespoons flour in 3 tablespoons oil
and dilute with water. Season with
salt, pepper and paprika.

CRAB SAUCE WITH SPAGHETTI

1 lb. fresh crab or canned crab meat
1/2 cup chopped onion
1/2 cup chopped celery
2 cloves garlic, finely chopped
2 tbsps. chopped parsley
1/4 cup margarine, melted
1 cup canned tomatoes
1 can (8 ozs.) tomato sauce
1/4 tsp. salt
1/2 tsp. paprika
Dash pepper
3 cups cooked spaghetti

1. Cut crab meat into 1/2-inch pieces.
2. Cook onion, celery, garlic and parsley in margarine until tender.
3. Add tomatoes, tomato sauce and seasonings. Simmer for 20 minutes, stirring occasionally.
4. Add crab meat, heat. Serve over spaghetti.
(Yield: 6 servings)

CLAM SAUCE WITH SPAGHETTI

4 doz. medium fresh clams (save water from cooked clams)
1 cup chopped onion
4 to 5 cloves garlic, minced
1/2 cup chopped parsley
1/2 cup margarine
1 tsp. salt
1 tsp. dried basil leaves
Freshly ground pepper to taste
2 tbsps. salt
4 to 6 quarts boiling water
1 lb. spaghetti

1. Wash clams thoroughly. In large pot, cook covered in small amount of water just until clams open. Remove clams. Strain the broth and reserve 3 cups. Remove clams from shells; chop.

2. In large skillet or dutch oven saute onion, garlic and parsley in melted margarine until onion is almost tender; add clams, reserved broth, 1 teaspoon salt, basil and pepper. Boil 1 minute.

3. Meanwhile, add 2 tablespoons salt to rapidly boiling water. Gradually add spaghetti so that water continues to boil. Cook uncovered, stirring occasionally, until tender. Drain in colander. Serve in shallow bowls topped with clam sauce. Yield: 8 servings.

NOTE: If you do not have fresh clams, use 2 cups canned minced clams and 3 cups bottled clam juice.

DOLMADES

1 jar grape leaves
2 tbsps. dried mint
Juice of 3 lemons
2 cups water
2 tsps. salt
1/4 tsp. pepper
2 cups rice, long-grain
1 tbsp. chopped dill
1 cup olive or vegetable oil
2 large onions or 1 bunch green onions, chopped fine

Place grape leaves in bowl of warm water for about 15 minutes before using. Combine rice, oil, water, onions, seasonings and juice of 2 lemons in a saucepan. Place over high heat, stirring constantly until mixture comes to a boil. Lower heat and simmer until most of the liquid is absorbed. Remove from fire. Place 1 tsp. of rice mixture in center of grape leaf, and roll, folding in sides. Arrange in layers in deep saucepan, adding 3 tbsps. oil, juice of 1 lemon, and enough water to cover rolls. Place a heavy plate over rolls. Cover saucepan and cook slowly until most of the liquid is absorbed and rice is tender. Additional water may be added if necessary.

STUFFED GREEN PEPPERS

6 green peppers, medium size
2 large onions, chopped fine
1/4 cup chopped dill
1/2 cup chopped parsley
1/2 cup raisins (optional)
1/4 tsp. pepper
1 1/2 cups rice
1/2 cup chopped celery
1/2 cup vegetable oil
1 1/2 tsp. salt

Saute onion, celery, and seasonings in
vegetable oil until soft and transparent.
Add rice, which has been washed and rinsed
well. Stir lightly until slightly brown;
add 1/2 cup water. Cover, lower heat, and
cook until liquid is absorbed. (Rice will
be partially cooked). Cut a slice from
stem end of pepper, and carefully remove
seeds. Rinse in cold water. Fill with
rice mixture, and replace top slice.
Place in baking pan with 1 cup water, 1
tablespoon oil and 3 tablespoons tomato
sauce. Bake in oven, 375 degrees, for
about 1 hour, basting occasionally.

VARIATION: For tomato flavor in stuffing,
add 2 cups tomatoes, or 3 tablespoons
tomato paste in 1/2 cup water, and simmer
with onions before adding rice.

NOTE: Medium-sized tomatoes also may be
stuffed with the above mixture.

GREENS AND BEAN CURD ORIENTAL STYLE

This very simple and satisfying dinner
dish is extremely quick to prepare once
the rice is boiled. First, boil as much
rice as your family uses for one meal.
The rice can be set aside with a lid on
it to get dry and fluffy while the rest
of the dinner cooks. Then, chop in bite-
size pieces, 10 ounces of Oriental Soy
Bean Curd. (This looks like milk curds,
and can be bought in Chinese or Japanese
stores, or health food stores. It is a
very mild, cheese-like substitute for
other protein foods which are forbidden
during Lent.) You will need a large a-
mount of greens of any three to five of
the following varieties. They should be
fresh and crisp.

Cabbage, onions, celery, turnips, daikon
(long, white radish), bean sprouts, bock
choy (Chinese greens), broccoli, napa cabbage, green peppers, swiss chard, mustard
greens, turnip greens, or collards.

Chop about 4 cupfuls of the greens (be
sure to include at least 1 onion) and set
aside. In a bowl, mix 1/4 cup soy sauce,
1/4 cup water and 2 tbsps. cornstarch until smooth. Now you are ready to begin.
In a large frying pan, heat 3 tbsps. oil
until almost smoking. Quickly add greens
to oil and stir and turn about 3 minutes,
until they are coated with oil and bright
green. Add the bean curd and the soy
sauce mixture. Stir rapidly until the
sauce thickens; only a few minutes, and
serve over fluffy white rice. The most
important thing in preparing this deli-
cacy is that the vegetables are only
partly cooked and still bright green and
crunchy.

MEXICAN HOMINY

1 medium onion, minced
1 medium green pepper, chopped
1/4 cup margarine
3 1/2 cups cooked hominy, drained
  (1 lb. 13-oz. can)
1 tsp. chili powder
1/2 tsp. salt
1/8 tsp. pepper

Cook onion and green pepper in the margarine in top pan of chafing dish over direct heat for about 10 minutes. Add remaining ingredients, and heat. Makes 4 servings.

LEEK CASSEROLE

1 1/2 lbs. leeks
1 cup oil
Paprika
Salt to taste
1/2 cup rice
1 can tomatoes
1 dried red pepper
1 cup water
1 lemon

Trim and clean the leeks, being careful to wash out all grit which is between the leaves. Cut leeks into 3-inch lengths. Parboil them being careful to keep them whole. Drain. Heat the oil, and gently fry the leeks for about 15 minutes. Place the leeks carefully in an ovenproof dish and place the rice, tomatoes and spices over them. Cover with water and bake in a 375-degree oven until the rice is cooked. Just before serving, squeeze lemon juice over the dish.

LENTIL FRY

Season 1 cup of cooked lentils and 1 cup
of cooked, diced potatoes with onion salt.
Fry in margarine. Serve with chili sauce.

LENTIL SOUP

1 pkg. lentils (1 lb.)
1 medium-size onion
5 or 6 garlic cloves
Salt and pepper to taste
Water

Bring lentils to rolling boil in 8 cups
water. Continue boiling for 5 more
minutes. Remove from heat. Pass lentils
through wire sieve, removing all the
water. Add chopped onion, garlic cloves,
3 1/2 cups water, salt and pepper to lentils. Bring back to boil. Reduce heat
to simmer, cover and cook until done. If
water begins to evaporate, add 1/2 cup
more water. Remember, lentils should be
cooked so that a little water remains but
they should not appear pasty in appearance.
After you have used the recipe a few times,
you can easily judge the amount of liquid
that should remain.

LENTIL SOUP WITH TOMATOES

1 lb. lentils
1 can stewed tomatoes
2 chopped onions
2 cloves garlic, finely chopped
1/4 tsp. oregano or rosemary
Salt and pepper to taste

Cook lentils for 1 1/2 hours in plenty of
water. Fry the onions and garlic in oil
until the onions are golden and soft, and
add them and the tomatoes to the lentils.
Add spices and serve with bread or
crackers.

BAKED LENTILS

1 lb. (2 1/3 cups) lentils, washed
1 onion stuck with 3 whole cloves
1 bay leaf
5 cups water
2 tsps. salt

Combine in a Dutch oven or in top-of-the
range heat-proof cooking ware. Bring
water to boiling point. Cover; simmer 30
minutes. Without draining, stir in:

1/2 cup catsup
1/4 cup molasses
2 tbsps. brown sugar
1 tsp. dry mustard
1/4 tsp. Worchestershire sauce
2 tbsps. minced onion

Top with a little olive or vegetable oil
if desired. Cover and bake at 350 degrees
for 1 hour. Uncover last few minutes.
Leftover lentils can be refrigerated and
used as desired.

LENTILS WITH FRUIT

1 lb. (2 1/3 cups) lentils
5 cups water
2 tsps. salt
2 tbsps. Corn oil
4 tbsps. minced onion
1 fat clove garlic, minced
2 cans (8 ozs.) tomato sauce
2 medium-size cooked or canned sweet
  potatoes
2 firm fresh pears, peeled and cored
2 large slices canned pineapple
1 large firm banana, quite green
2 tsps. monosodium glutamate

Add washed lentils and salt to cold or
warm water in large heavy saucepan or
Dutch oven with tight-fitting cover.
Bring water to boiling point. Reduce
heat; cover. Simmer 30 minutes. Do
not drain. Slowly cook onions and garlic, in oil until onions are clear and
limp. Add tomato sauce. Cook a few
minutes, then stir into the lentils.
Cut sweet potatoes or yams, pears, pineapple in chunks; banana in 1/2-inch
slices. Add to lentils and sauce along
with monosodium glutamate. Simmer,
covered, until pears are tender, 15
minutes or more, stirring very carefully
occasionally.

NOTE: Canned pear halves cut in pieces
and canned pineapple chunks may be used.
Cooking time should be shortened. This
dish may be made ahead, as standing
blends the flavor. Heat slowly on range
surface unit or in moderate oven. Serve
hot.

E15

LIMA BEAN CASSEROLE

1 lb. large lima beans
8 medium onions
2 tsps. salt
4 large carrots
10 whole peppercorns
1/2 tsp. sugar

Soak beans. Change the water and cook
with one chopped onion for 1/2 hour. Add
salt. Slice onions and fry in 1/2 cup
oil. Slice carrots crosswise and add to
onions. Fry until browned slightly. Add
sugar. Place a layer of beans in a baking
dish. Then place a layer of fried vegetables over this, ending with vegetables.
Bake for 1 hour in 350-degree oven.

MINESTRONE MILANESE

1/4 cup olive oil (or other oil)
1 garlic clove, minced
1 onion, minced
1 leek, washed and diced (when in season)
1 tbsp. chopped parsley
1 tsp. dried thyme
1 tbsp. tomato paste
1/4 cup water
3 canned or fresh tomatoes, peeled,
  seeded, and chopped
3 celery stalks, chopped
2 carrots, diced
2 potatoes, diced
1/4 small cabbage, shredded
2 zucchini, diced
6 cups hot water
Salt to taste
1/2 tsp. pepper
1/3 cup uncooked rice
1 to 1 1/2 cups cooked and drained dried
  beans

Put oil in large kettle. Add garlic,
onion, leek, parsley and thyme and cook
until soft. Add tomato paste thinned
with 1/4 cup water and cook for 5
minutes. Add all remaining ingredients
except rice and beans. Simmer covered
for 1 hour. Bring to boil, add rice,
and cook until soft. Add beans; heat.
Makes 3 quarts or 6 servings.

MUSHROOM PILAF

1/2 cup chopped green onion
1 cup fresh mushrooms, halved or sliced
1/2 cup margarine
2 cups hot cooked white rice
2 cups hot cooked wild or brown rice

Cook onion and mushrooms in margarine
until soft, but not browned. Combine
with hot cooked white and wild rice.
Season to taste with salt and pepper.
Turn into heated serving dish and garnish with tomato slices and parsley.

PIROG (RUSSIAN COOKERY)

Make a lenten bread dough:
  2 cups warm (not hot) water
  3 tbsps. sugar
  2 tsps. salt
  1/3 cup oil
  1 envelope active dry yeast
  6 to 6 1/2 cups flour

Soften yeast in a large bowl in the warm
water. Add sugar, salt and oil and mix.
Add 3 cups flour and beat until smooth.
Add rest of flour to make soft dough.
Turn out on lightly floured board. Knead
until smooth and elastic.

Try to avoid adding more flour as the
dough should be light as possible. Cover,
let rise in warm place until doubled in
bulk (1 1/2 hours). Roll out very thin
on floured board and put in long flat pan.
The dough should be double the size of
the pan so it can be brought over to cover
the filling making a pie. Bake in 350-
degree oven until done. Cut in squares.
Best when hot but may be eaten cold, too.
Bake 25 to 30 minutes.

FILLING FOR PIROG:

Saute for 4 to 5 minutes medium chopped
onion in 2 to 3 tablespoons oil until
transparent. Add finely chopped cabbage
(which has been blanched with hot water)
and mix thoroughly. Add salt and pepper
to taste.

Mushrooms may be added to onions while
they are being sauteed for variety.

Chinese noodles and onions are a tasty
variety. Cook the noodles first according to package directions.

Uncooked red snapper or cod with the
onions also makes a tasty variation. Cook
in dough about 35 to 45 minutes.

NOTE: Leftover dough makes good lenten
cinnamon rolls using margarine and cinnamon with sugar.

PIZZA

Dilute in medium-sized bowl:

1 1/2 cakes yeast
1 cup water
1 tsp. sugar

Add and knead together:

1/3 cup salad oil
3 1/2 cups flour

Mix a little shortening with dough
(about 1/4 cup) and knead until satiny.
Let rise in warm place (about 15
minutes).

Brown 1 medium onion, chopped, in 1/4
cup oil until golden. Add 1 can shrimp
(if desired) and 1 can mushrooms,
drained. Turn heat off. Add tomato
topping. Grease a long pan and put
dough in the pan and spread it out with
your fingers. (Grease your fingers
with shortening for easier handling of
the dough. Spread the topping over the
dough. Bake at 375 degrees for 20 to
30 minutes.

TOMATO TOPPING:

1 cup tomato sauce
1/2 tsp. salt
1 tsp. Worcestershire sauce
1/4 tsp. chili powder
1/2 tsp. prepared mustard
1/2 tsp. paprika
1/2 to 3/4 tsp. garlic salt
Oregano to taste

POTATO SOUP

4 potatoes, cubed
1 carrot
1 small onion, diced
1 stalk celery, with leaf
1 tsp. parsley leaves

In 2 quarts water, place carrot, parsley and celery and onion. Boil 15 minutes. Add potatoes and boil 10 to 14 minutes more. In frying pan, put 2 tablespoons oil and 1 tablespoon flour. Fry to a dark brown, add small onion, fry 10 minutes, stirring constantly. Add 1 teaspoon caraway seed and 1/2 cup water and boil 10 minutes. Strain and add to soup and season to taste.

POTATO STEW

2 chopped onions
1/2 chopped green pepper
1 fresh tomato, or 1/2 cup canned
  tomatoes
5 or 6 cubed potatoes
1 stalk celery, chopped

Fry onion, celery, green pepper in 2 tablespoons oil. Add salt, pepper and paprika to taste. Add cubed potatoes, 1/4 cup water and tomatoes. Simmer until potatoes are done.

BRAZILIAN RICE

3 cups boiling water
2 cups uncooked brown rice
1 tsp. salt
3 tbsps. margarine
1 tsp. chili powder
1/8 tsp. garlic powder
1 tsp. brown sugar
1 tsp. grated orange peel
1 cup sliced Brazilnuts or almonds
1 can (2 1/4 oz.) sliced black olives

To boiling water add rice, salt, margarine, chili powder, garlic powder,
sugar, and orange peel; stir, cover,
reduce heat, and cook for 20 minutes.
Remove from heat and add nuts and
olives; mix lightly. Remove to serving
plate. Serves 8.

SPANISH RICE

1/4 cup oil
1 cup uncooked rice
1/2 cup onion, finely chopped
1 can tomato sauce
2 cups water
1 1/2 tsps. salt
1 tsp. sugar
1/2 tsp. chili powder
1/2 cup green pepper, chopped
1/2 cup celery, diced

Heat oil in heavy 10-inch skillet. Add
rice; cook, stirring over medium heat until golden. Add onion, cook 1 minute.
Add tomato sauce, water, seasonings,
green pepper and celery. Cover, cook over
low heat for 25 minutes or longer until
rice is tender. Stir occasionally. (1
can shrimp, drained, can be added and
cooked just to heat shrimp if desired).

SOYBEAN SHEPHERDS PIE

12 small white onions, peeled
4 carrots, halved crosswise
2 cups cooked soybeans
2 tbsps. all-purpose flour
2 tbsps. margarine
1 tsp. salt
1/8 tsp. pepper
3 cups seasoned mashed potatoes

Cover onions with water and cook, covered,
for 20 minutes. Add carrots, cover and
cook 10 minutes longer, or until tender.
Drain, reserving liquid. Put onion,
carrots, and beans in 2-quart casserole.
Brown flour lightly in the margarine.
Gradually add 2 cups reserved vegetable
liquid and salt. Cook 2 minutes; add
pepper and pour liquid over vegetables.
Spread potatoes on top. Bake for 15 to
20 minutes at 425 degrees.

LENTEN-STYLE SPAGHETTI

2 stalks celery
1 medium onion
1/2 medium green pepper (if desired)
1 or 2 cloves garlic
1 tsp. oregano
1 1/2 tsp. salt
1 bay leaf
1/2 tsp. pepper
2 tbsps. sugar
1 tsp. basil
1/4 tsp. cinnamon
1 can tomato sauce (8 oz.)
2 cans tomato paste (6 oz. each)
2 1-lb. cans tomatoes

Chop celery, onion, green pepper (if desired), and garlic. Brown in skillet with about 3 tbsps. oil. When browned, sprinkle with the oregano, salt, bay leaf, pepper, sugar, basil, and cinnamon. Then add tomato sauce, tomato paste and tomatoes. Let all simmer slowly for 3 or 4 hours. The longer the better. Let it get thick and dark. Stir occasionally. Mix with cooked, drained spaghetti.

VARIATION: For a hot, spicy spaghetti sauce, add 1/4 tsp. of each of the following with the other seasonings: cloves, allspice, paprika, chili powder, thyme, and rosemary.

NOTE: This sauce can be frozen.

SPAGHETTI WITH GARBANZO SAUCE

1 onion, chopped
1 garlic clove, minced
1/2 cup celery and tops, chopped
3 tbsps. olive or vegetable oil
2 cups undrained garbanzo beans
  (1 lb. 3-oz. can)
2 1/3 cups tomatoes (1 lb. 3-oz. can)
1 can tomato paste (6-oz. can)
1 bay leaf
1 tsp. salt
Dash of cayenne
1/2 tsp. ground oregano
1 lb. spaghetti, cooked

Saute onion, garlic, and celery in oil until golden. Drain garbanzos, reserving liquid. Measure liquid; add water to make 2 1/2 cups. Add with garbanzos, tomatoes, tomato paste, bay leaf, and seasonings to onion mixture. Simmer, uncovered, for 2 hours, stirring occasionally. Serve on spaghetti. Makes 8 servings.

SPAGHETTI WITH ZUCCHINI SAUCE

1/4 cup margarine
1/2 cup finely diced onion
1/4 cup finely diced green pepper
1 lb. zucchini squash, sliced
2 cups diced fresh tomatoes
1 tsp. salt
1/8 tsp. pepper
1 can sliced mushrooms (4 ozs.)
8 ozs. spaghetti

Melt margarine over low heat; add onion and saute for 2 minutes. Add green pepper, squash, tomatoes, salt, pepper, and undrained mushrooms. Cover and cook over low heat for about 40 minutes. Cook spaghetti according to package directions. Drain in colander. Serve hot sauce over spaghetti.

SPINACH RICE

1 lb. spinach
1 tbsp. chopped dill
1/4 cup olive or vegetable oil
Salt and pepper to taste
1 chopped onion
2/3 cup rice
1 1/2 cups water

Saute onions in oil until soft. Wash spinach several times, drain well and chop. Add to onions, and simmer slowly until almost cooked. Add water, bring to boiling point, stir in rice and seasonings. Cover and simmer for 15 minutes, or until rice is soft and liquid is absorbed. Add juice of a half lemon before removing rice from heat.

VARIATION: For tomato flavor, omit lemon juice and add 1/2 cup tomato sauce to sauteed onions.

E24

STUFFED TOMATOES

10 large tomatoes
1 cup rice
1 onion, chopped
5 cloves garlic, minced
1/4 cup dill, chopped
Salt and pepper
1/4 cup parsley, chopped
1/4 cup tomato paste
1/4 cup water
1/2 cup oil
1 tbsp. sugar
2 cups pulp and juice scooped from
  tomatoes

Slice tops from tomatoes and scoop out
centers. Discard hard center. Place in
baking pan. Mix all ingredients together and spoon into tomato cups. Replace tops. Pour in enough boiling
water to cover bottom of pan. Cover and
bake at 350 degrees for about 45 minutes,
then uncover and bake until brown and
done.

VEGETABLE SOUP

3 large potatoes
1/2 cup celery, chopped
1 small onion, sliced thin
Pepper
2 tbsps. rice
2 tbsps. tomato paste
3 carrots
4 tbsps. oil
1 tsp. salt
2 cups tomatoes
2 cups water
Chopped parsley

Prepare vegetables and cut in cubes of
uniform size. Cook celery and onions
slowly in oil for 10 minutes. Add remaining ingredients and boil until vegetables
are soft, about 1 hour. Add more water,
if needed. This should be a thick soup.

VEGETABLE STOCK

1/4 cup margarine
2 medium onions, diced
3 medium carrots, diced
1 medium turnip, diced
1 celery stalk, diced
1 small head of lettuce, diced
2 large tomatoes, peeled and quartered
1 bay leaf
8 parsley sprigs
1 thyme sprig
8 peppercorns, crushed slightly
1 garlic clove
2 whole cloves
2 vegetable bouillon cubes
1 1/2 quarts boiling water
1 tsp. monosodium glutamate

Heat margarine in kettle. Add next 5
ingredients and cook very slowly, covered,
for about 25 minutes, stirring frequently.
Add remaining ingredients except monosodium glutamate. Simmer, covered, for
about 1 1/2 hours, skimming as skum rises
to the top. Add monosodium glutamate.
Strain through cheesecloth and store in
refrigerator. Makes about 1 1/2 quarts
stock.

S A L A D S, S A U C E S
A N D M A R I N A D E S

Salads:

ARTICHOKE HEARTS SALAD

1 pkg. frozen artichoke hearts (9 ozs.)
1 medium head lettuce, shredded
1 cup small raw cauliflowerettes
1 large tomato, diced
1 tbsp. chopped chives
2 large ripe olives, sliced
2 large stuffed olives, sliced
2 tbsps. chopped dill pickle
French dressing (oil and vinegar,
  seasoned)

Cook artichokes as directed on package.
Chill. Lightly toss vegetables, olives
and pickle with dressing to moisten.
Serve at once.

ARTICHOKE AND ONION SALAD

6 artichokes
1/2 cup salad oil
1 tsp. salt
1/2 cup chopped green onions
6 small onions
1 cup water
Dash of pepper
2 lemons
Chopped parsley, marjoram, dill

Prepare artichokes by breaking off about
3 or 4 rows of the outside petals that
stand out, leaving the fleshy portion at
the bottom. Cut around the broken petals
with a sharp knife to remove any of the
tough portions. Rub the cut portions of
the artichokes immediately with lemon to
prevent discoloring. Cut off the tough
parts of the leaves about 2 inches from
the stem. Take out the reddish prickly
center with a spoon and scoop out the fuzz
underneath, being careful not to dig into
the meaty flesh of the artichoke itself.

F3

Rub all over with lemon. Peel the skin
off the stem and cut, leaving about 1/2
inch. Let stand in salted water until
ready to cook. Place a small peeled
white onion in the center of each artichoke. Place, cut side down, in an enamel
saucepan. Add the seasonings, water, oil,
green onions, and the juice of 1 lemon.
Cover; simmer 45 minutes until artichokes
are tender. When they are cooked, sprinkle
with chopped parsley, marjoram and dill.
Simmer another 5 minutes. Serve cold with
a lemon and oil dressing.

SESAME ASPARAGUS SALAD

1 pkg. frozen cut asparagus (10 ozs.)
1 head romaine, broken in pieces
2 pimientos, diced
1 green onion, chopped
1/4 cup toasted sesame seed
1/4 tsp. cracked pepper
1/4 tsp. herb seasoning
2 tbsps. each of lemon juice and salad
  oil
Salt to taste

Cook, drain, and chill asparagus. Add
to next 3 ingredients. Mix sesame seed,
pepper, herb seasoning, lemon juice, and
oil. Add to first mixture; toss. Add
salt.

AVOCADO-CITRUS SALAD

Halve unpeeled avocados and remove seeds.
Sprinkle avocados with lemon juice and
fill cavity with grapefruit or orange segments. Add honey to taste and garnish
with fresh mint.

FOUR BEAN SALAD

1 can garbanzo beans
1 can wax beans
1 can green beans
1 can kidney beans
1 onion, sliced or chopped
1 green pepper, chopped
1/2 cup salad oil
1/2 cup sugar
1/2 cup wine vinegar
Salt to taste

Mix oil, vinegar and sugar together.
Add salt to taste. Drain beans and add
to first mixture. Toss lightly with
onions and green peppers. This should
marinate at least 24 hours and can marinate several days. Stir several times
while it marinates. To serve, drain all
the dressing off and pour the beans into a lettuce-lined bowl.

STRING BEAN SALAD

2 lbs. fresh string beans, frenched
1 tbsp. salt
1/2 onion, chopped fine
Parsley leaves, chopped
2 tbsps. salad oil
1/2 cup vinegar
1 tbsp. prepared mustard

Bring to a boil 2 quarts water, add salt
and beans. Cook until beans are soft,
about 1/2 hour. Strain beans and cool.
Add onion and parsley and mix. Make
dressing of the salad oil, vinegar and
mustard and pour over bean mixture.

SWEET-SOUR BEAN SALAD

2 cans cut green beans (1 lb. each)
1 can garbanzo beans (1-lb. can)
1 can pimiento, diced
1 sweet red onion
1 clove garlic
1 tsp. salt
1/2 cup cider vinegar
1/2 cup tarragon wine vinegar
2/3 cup sugar
1/2 cup salad oil
Pepper to taste

Drain and rinse beans. Combine with
pimiento and onion sliced into thin rings.
Crush garlic into salt; combine with rest
of ingredients in glass jar. Cover and
shake until well-blended. Pour over
salad. Cover with foil and marinate in
refrigerator overnight or several days.
Flavor seems to improve. Stir occasionally. Heap into shallow salad bowl or
drain and serve on crisp lettuce. Serves 6.

CAULIFLOWER SALAD

1 head cauliflower
1/4 cup oil
3 tbsps. vinegar
1/8 tsp. sugar
Salt

Wash cauliflower. Place in bowl of salted
water, head down, and allow to stand for
about 1/2 hour. Rewash, separate and place
in boiling, salted water. Cook until tender in covered pan. Do not overcook.
Strain, cool, place in salad bowl and add
balance of ingredients which have been
blended together. If desired, more vinegar may be added.
NOTE: Asparagus may be substituted for
cauliflower.

CORN AND LIMA BEAN SALAD

1 pkg. frozen cut corn (10 ozs.)
1 pkg. frozen lima beans (10 ozs.)
1 tsp. salt
Dash pepper
1 tbsp. vinegar
1 tsp. instant minced onion
2 cups sliced celery
2 pimientos sliced
French dressing (oil and vinegar)
Salad greens

Cook corn and beans as directed on labels.
Drain and add salt and pepper. Cool.
Add next 4 ingredients and moisten with
dressing. Chill and serve on greens.

CRANBERRY SALAD

1 lb. cranberries
2 apples peeled
1 large orange
1 cup chopped nuts
1 1/2 cups sugar
2 pkgs. cherry jello (kosher)

Grind all ingredients together. Then
add nuts, sugar and jello. (Juice is
used for the cold part of the jello.)
Stir together and chill.

CRANBERRY JELLO

1 quart cranberry juice cocktail (4 cups)
2 pkgs. lemon jello (kosher)
1/2 tsp. grated orange peel
1 unpeeled red apple, diced
1 cup celery, chopped fine
1 can mandarin oranges

Heat 2 cups cranberry juice, dissolve
jello in juice; add grated orange peel
and rest of juice (2 cups). Chill until
partially set and fold in fruit and
celery. Chill until firm.

FRUIT SALAD

1 can fruit cocktail, drained
1 can mandarin oranges, drained
2 bananas, sliced
1 cup small marshmallows
Coconut (if desired)
Non-dairy Cool Whip

Put all ingredients in a large salad
bowl and add enough Cool Whip to coat
all.

FRUIT SALAD BOWL

2 grapefruits
4 oranges
1 avocado
Salad greens
Juice of 1 lemon
1/4 cup salad oil
1 can frozen concentrated tangerine
   juice (6-oz. can)

Section grapefruits and oranges. Peel,
pit, and slice avocado. Put in bowl with
salad greens. Refrigerate while dressing is being made. Put lemon juice, oil,
and tangerine juice in blender. Whirl
until well-mixed. Pour over salad greens
and toss lightly. Makes 4 to 6 servings.

FRUIT AND SHRIMP BOAT

1 lb. shrimp, cooked and deveined
3 cups assorted melon balls, drained
1 cup pineapple chunks, drained
3/4 cup Russian dressing (bottled)

In large bowl, combine shrimp, melon
balls, pineapple chunks, and Russian
dressing; cover and refrigerate at least
1 hour. Mound in melon baskets or pineapple shells. May also be spooned into
individual lettuce cups. Makes 6 to 8
servings.

LENTIL SALAD

2 cups dried lentils
1/8 tsp. salt
1 onion stuck with 2 cloves
1 bay leaf
6 scallions, chopped
1 cup chopped parsley
1/2 cup French dressing (oil and vinegar)
Salt and pepper
Salad greens
Red pepper strips

Wash lentils and boil for 2 minutes in
water to cover. Remove from heat, cover,
and let stand for 1 hour. Add the salt,
onion, and bay leaf. Bring again to a
boil. Lower heat and simmer, covered,
until lentils are tender. Do not overcook. Drain and cool. Combine lentils
with scallions, parsley, and French
dressing. Season with salt and pepper to
taste. Toss thoroughly. Chill before
serving. Serve on salad greens and garnish with strips of red pepper. Makes
4 to 6 servings.

ORANGE AND ENDIVE SALAD

4 navel oranges
8 heads Belgian endive
3/4 cup olive or vegetable oil
1/4 cup mild cider vinegar
1 tsp. salt
2 tsps. mild prepared mustard
1/4 cup fresh orange juice

Peel oranges and remove all white membrane. Separate sections and remove seeds
and membrane between sections. Chill.
Cut endive into rounds and chill. Make
dressing by combining remaining ingredients. Chill. At serving time, combine
oranges and endive. Stir dressing well
and toss salad in it.

ORANGE-BANANA SALAD

6 oranges
3 bananas
Sugar

Peel and section oranges. Slice sections
into bite-size pieces. Put in bowl with
sliced bananas. Sprinkle on sugar to
taste and fold together until sugar dissolves and banana slices are all coated
with orange juice.

ORIENTAL SALAD

Potatoes
Oil
Salt and pepper
Vinegar
Garlic
Dried onions or green onions
String beans (boiled)
Parsley leaves
Radishes

Boil potatoes in jackets, peel and slice
thinly while still hot. Pour dressing
over them, made from oil, salt, pepper
and vinegar. Add onions which have been
cut thin or minced. Add green beans
which have been cut in small pieces,
crushed garlic, parsley leaves cut fine
(optional). Sliced radishes or minced
mustard greens can be added for flavor.
Celery, green pepper, black olives, can
be varied according to taste.

POTATO SALAD

4 potatoes, diced
1 onion, finely chopped
Oregano or parsley
1/4 cup olive or vegetable oil
Juice of 1 lemon
Salt and pepper

Boil potatoes until tender; cut in small
pieces. Add lemon juice and oil, sprinkle
with chopped parsley or oregano. Toss
lightly. Serve warm or cold.

STRAWBERRY GELATIN SALAD

1 large pkg. strawberry jello (kosher)
1 large pkg. frozen strawberries

Add 2 cups boiling water to jello and
dissolve. Add frozen strawberries and
stir until you can separate berries with
a fork. Refrigerate until firm.

NOTE: This is also good with raspberry
jello and frozen raspberries.

TOMATO-CUCUMBER SALAD

2 large cucumbers	vinegar
2 large tomatoes	water
1 onion, sliced	sugar
	pepper

Slice cucumbers and onion. Soak in salt
water for 20 to 30 minutes. Mix dressing
of vinegar, water, sugar and pepper in
jar and shake well. (Amount of ingredients in dressing depend on your own
taste.) Drain salt water from cucumbers
and add dressing and tomatoes cut into
eighths.

SLICED TOMATO SALAD

2 large or 4 medium ripe tomatoes, peeled
1/2 medium sweet white onion
1/2 thumb-sized piece fresh ginger root
1 tbsp. sugar
1/8 tsp. pepper
1/2 tsp. salt
1/2 tsp. monosodium glutamate
2 tbsps. red wine vinegar
Lettuce leaves and chopped parsley

Slice the tomatoes about 1/4-inch thick.
Cut onion in thin slices. Peel the ginger
root, cut in very thin slices, then cut
each slice into thin strips. In a shallow
serving bowl, alternate slices of tomato
and onion, distributing the ginger evenly.
Combine sugar, pepper, salt, monosodium
glutamate, and vinegar; stir until sugar
is dissolved, then pour over tomatoes.
Cover the bowl and chill for about 2
hours. Just before serving, spoon some
of the marinade from the bowl over tomatoes. Garnish with lettuce leaves and
sprinkle top with parsley.

WESTERN SALAD

1 9-oz. pkg. frozen artichoke hearts
1/2 cup salad oil
1/4 cup lemon juice
3 tbsps. tarragon vinegar
2 tbsps. sugar
2 tbsps. minced onion
1 clove garlic, crushed
1 tsp. salt
1/2 tsp. dry mustard
Freshly ground black pepper
3 heads Bibb or 2 heads red leaf lettuce
   or combination of both
2 medium heads Romaine lettuce
1/2 bunch radishes
1 avocado
1 cup packaged croutons
2 tbsps. margarine

Cook artichokes according to package directions; drain well. Combine next 9 ingredients in jar; cover and shake. Pour small amount of dressing over artichokes. Cover and chill several hours. Slice avocado and place in small bowl. Sprinkle small amount of dressing on avocado. Cover well and chill. In small skillet brown croutons in margarine until toasted on all sides. Tear greens in small bite-sized pieces and layer with paper towels in large bowl or other container; cover with damp cloth and refrigerate.

To serve salad, fluff crisp dry greens into salad bowl; add artichokes, dressing and sliced radishes. Toss. Season with salt and freshly ground pepper. Add avocado and warm croutons; toss gently. Makes 8 servings.

BARBECUE SAUCE

1 cup catsup
1/2 cup honey
1 tbsp. Worcestershire sauce
1/2 cup margarine
Juice of 1 lemon
1 clove garlic, minced
1/2 tsp. cumin powder
Salt and pepper

Bring all ingredients to a boil.
Simmer for 20 minutes.

MARINER'S SAUCE

3 garlic cloves, minced
1/4 cup minced parsley
1/2 cup olive or vegetable oil
2 cups chopped, peeled tomatoes
1 tsp. crumbled dried oregano
Salt and pepper to taste

Saute garlic and parsley in oil. When
garlic is delicately brown, add tomatoes,
oregano, salt, pepper, and simmer for
30 minutes, or until well-blended and
thick. Makes about 1 1/2 cups.

PARSLEY-OLIVE SAUCE

1/2 cup margarine
1/2 cup chopped parsley
1 cup green olives, pitted and chopped
1/4 tsp. pepper
8 ozs. spaghetti, cooked
Salt to taste

Melt margarine. Add parsley, olives, and
pepper. Pour over spaghetti, toss, and
add salt to taste. Makes 4 servings.

SAUCES FOR FISH

Brown Butter:
Brown slowly, but do not burn, 1/4 cup
margarine, stirring constantly. Add 2
teaspoons fresh lemon juice and 1/4
teaspoon salt.

Chili:
Heat 1/4 cup margarine. Add 2 tablespoons chili sauce and 1 tablespoon
fresh lemon juice.

Creole:
Cook 1/2 cup chopped onion and 1 minced
garlic clove in 3 tablespoons cooking oil
until yellow. Add 1/2 cup chopped green
pepper, 1 bay leaf, 2 1/3 cups (1 lb. 3
oz. can) tomatoes, 1 teaspoon salt, 1/8
teaspoon pepper and a dash of cayenne.
Simmer for 20 minutes.

Garlic or Onion Vinegar:
Rub together 1 minced garlic clove or 1/2
medium onion, 1 teaspoon sugar, and 1/2
teaspoon paprika. Add 1/2 cup hot vinegar. Cool and strain.

Green:
Slowly cook together 1/2 cup olive or
vegetable oil, 1 minced garlic clove, 1/3
cup minced parsley, 2 tablespoons minced
green onion tops and 1/2 teaspoon salt
for 5 minutes. Add 2 chopped raw spinach
leaves.

Herb and Wine Vinegar:
Heat to boiling 1/2 cup wine vinegar, 1
onion slice, 1/2 bay leaf, and 1/4 teaspoon each of ground thyme and sage.
Cool, strain.

Hot Cocktail:
Combine 1 cup chili sauce, 3 drops of hot
pepper sauce, 2 tablespoons fresh lemon
juice, 1 teaspoon salt, 1/4 teaspoon
pepper, 1 teaspoon Worcestershire sauce,
1 tablespoon prepared horseradish, and
2 tablespoons pickle relish.

Mushroom Sherry:
Cook 1/2 cup minced fresh mushrooms and
1 tablespoon minced onion in 1/4 cup
margarine until tender. Add 1/2 teaspoon
salt and 2 tablespoons sherry.

Parsley, Chervil, or Chive Sauce:
Heat 1/4 cup margarine and 2 tablespoons
minced parsley or chervil, or 1 tablespoon
minced chives.

Pimiento:
Heat 1/4 cup margarine and 1 minced
pimiento.

Savory:
Cream 1/3 cup margarine until fluffy. Add
1 tablespoon each of minced green onion
tops or chives, celery leaves, and parsley,
dash of garlic salt, 1/2 teaspoon salt,
1/2 teaspoon sage.

Soy Butter:
Heat together 3 tablespoons margarine and
3 tablespoons soy sauce.

SKORDALIA OR GARLIC SAUCE

1 small potato
3 garlic cloves, minced
1 tsp. salt
1 cup olive or vegetable oil
1/3 cup vinegar

Peel potato and boil until tender. Put
through a sieve. Measure 1/2 cup potato
and place in a bowl; mix in garlic and
salt. Gradually add oil and vinegar
alternately while beating with a spoon.
Chill. Makes about 1 1/4 cups.

SWEET 'N SOUR SAUCE FOR SHRIMP

1 cup sugar
1/2 cup white vinegar
1/2 cup water
1 tbsp. chopped green pepper
1 tbsp. chopped pimiento
1 tsp. paprika
1/2 tsp. salt
3 tsps. cornstarch (more if you like it
    thicker)
1 tbsp. cold water
Pineapple chunks may be added if desired

Combine sugar, vinegar, 1/2 cup water,
green pepper, pimiento, paprika and salt.
Boil 5 minutes. Blend cornstarch and
water; add to syrup and cook until
thickened. Add pineapple chunks if
desired.

BASIC TOMATO SAUCE

1/4 cup minced onion
1 garlic clove, minced (optional)
1/4 cup olive or vegetable oil
1/4 cup minced raw carrot
1 cup minced celery
1/4 cup minced sweet basil
Salt and pepper to taste
3 cups canned tomato sauce or two 6 oz.
    cans tomato paste diluted with 3 cans
    water

Saute onion and garlic in oil until golden
brown. Add carrot, celery, sweet basil,
and salt and pepper, and continue cooking
until vegetables are wilted. Add tomato
sauce and simmer for 45 minutes, until
tasty and thick. Serve this sauce over
spaghetti or rice. Makes about 2 3/4
cups.

TOMATO PUREE SAUCE

2 tbsps. chopped parsley
1/4 cup margarine
1 can tomato puree (10 1/2 oz.)
1 tbsp. water
8 ozs. spaghetti, cooked

Saute parsley in margarine for 2 minutes.
Add tomato puree and water; heat. Serve
on spaghetti. Makes 4 servings.

TOMATO SAUCE FOR SPAGHETTI

1 garlic clove, minced
1 green pepper, minced
1/3 cup chopped celery
1 large onion, chopped
3 parsley sprigs
2 medium carrots, diced
2 tbsps. olive or vegetable oil
2 1/2 cups chopped fresh or canned
   tomatoes
2 bay leaves
6 peppercorns
1/4 tsp. thyme
2 tsps. salt
Dash of cayenne
6 whole cloves
1 tbsp. sugar
1 can tomato paste
1/2 lb. mushrooms, sliced
1 tbsp. margarine

Put first 7 ingredients in kettle. Cover
and cook gently for 15 minutes; do not
brown. Stir frequently. Add remaining
ingredients except tomato paste, mushrooms, and margarine and simmer, covered,
for about 45 minutes. Force through a
coarse sieve or food mill. Add tomato
paste. Saute mushrooms in the margarine
for about 5 minutes. Add to sauce, and
heat. Makes enough sauce for 12 ounces
of spaghetti or 4 servings.

WALNUT SAUCE

In heavy saucepan mix 1 cup light corn
syrup, 1/8 teaspoon salt, 1/4 cup water,
and if desired, 1/4 teaspoon maple flavoring. Add 1 1/4 cups coarsley chopped
walnuts. Bring to boil, cover; simmer
for about 25 minutes. Cool, and cover
tightly. Refrigerate. Makes about 2
cups. Good on gingerbread or cakes.

WHITE TUNA SAUCE

1 onion, chopped
1 garlic clove, chopped
1/4 cup oil or vegetable oil
2 cans tuna fish (7 oz. each)
1/2 tsp. pepper
8 ozs. spaghetti, cooked
Salt to taste

Saute onion and garlic in oil until golden. Add tuna, and simmer for 5 minutes.
Add pepper. Pour over spaghetti. Toss,
and add salt. Makes 4 servings.

UNCOOKED MARINADES

Fruit:
    1/3 cup sweet vermouth
    3/4 cup olive or vegetable oil
    1/4 tsp. salt
    1 tbsp. light corn syrup
    1 tsp. minced fresh tarragon or 1/4
        tsp. dried tarragon
    Freshly ground pepper to taste

Combine all ingredients and shake well in
a jar. Makes about 1 cup.

Shrimps or Lobster:
    3/4 cup brandy, dry sherry, or dry
        white wine
    1/2 tsp. salt
    1/2 tsp. pepper
    1/2 tsp. crushed dried rosemary, basil,
        or thyme

Combine all ingredients and put in deep
bowl. Marinate seafood in mixture for
1 to 3 hours. Makes about 3/4 cup or
enough for 30 shrimps or one 2-pound
lobster.

Vegetables:
    1 cup highly seasoned French dressing
        (oil and vinegar)
    2 tbsps. chopped chives
    1 garlic clove
    Few sprigs of parsley, chopped
    2 tsps. mixed dried herbs (mint,
        tarragon, basil)

Mix all ingredients, cover and store in
the refrigerator. Remove garlic. Use as
a marinade for tomatoes, green beans,
broccoli, asparagus, or other vegetables.
Makes 1 cup.

S H E L L F I S H

MOLDED BEANS, SHRIMPS AND RICE

1 can cut green beans (1-lb. can)
2 tbsps. oil
2 tbsps. lemon juice
1 or 2 cloves garlic, minced
1 tsp. salt
1/8 tsp. pepper
1/3 cup ripe olives, chopped
1/4 cup minced parsley
2 tbsps. sliced green onions
3 cups cooked rice, cooled
1/2 lb. cooked, shelled fresh tiny
    shrimp or 2 cans (4 1/2 ozs. each)
    shrimp, drained
Pink sauce (recipe below)

Drain beans, cut crosswise in half. Combine beans in a large bowl with all remaining ingredients, except Pink Sauce, tossing well. Pack firmly into 5 1/2-or 6-cup mold. Refrigerate several hours. Invert onto plate. Serve with Pink Sauce.

PINK SAUCE: Blend 1/2 cup non-dairy sour cream (IMO) with 1/4 cup chili sauce, 1/4 cup catsup and 2 tsps. dill weed. Chill.

CLAM CHOWDER

1/4 cup oil
1 1/2 cups minced onion
2 cans baby clams (8 ozs. each, drained,)
  (Put liquid aside for later use)
2 cups celery, cut small
2 cups potatoes, diced
1/3 cup green pepper, diced
1/4 tsp. garlic salt or minced garlic
2/3 cup canned or fresh tomatoes
1/4 cup tomato sauce
2 cups water
(Optional--1/2 cup green onions, 1 tbsp.
 dry parsley or small diced carrots)

Cook onion in oil until golden brown; add
clams and simmer for about 5 minutes; add
celery and let it simmer for a few minutes,
then add green onions (if desired), green
pepper, parsley, carrots, garlic and simmer for a few minutes stirring constantly.
Add tomatoes, tomato sauce and simmer for
5 minutes; then add clam liquid, water,
salt and pepper to taste. Cook for half
hour, then add diced potatoes. Cook additional half hour or until all vegetables
are done.

NOTE: The vegetables you use in this recipe can vary. If you have no green
peppers, substitute carrots. Use the
vegetables that your family likes to eat
the best. Serve this with Lenten bread-
sticks or French bread. It is delicious.

CLAM HASH

4 cups diced cold boiled potatoes
1/2 cup diced cooked carrots
1 onion, chopped
1/4 tsp. crushed thyme
1 can minced clams (10 1/2 oz.)
3 tbsps. margarine
Salt and pepper

Mix first 4 ingredients and undrained
clams. Let stand about 20 minutes to
allow clam liquid to soak into vegetables.
Heat margarine in skillet and add mixture. Cook slowly, turning occasionally,
until lightly browned. Season to taste.

CLAM SOUP, ITALIAN STYLE

1/4 cup olive or vegetable oil
4 slices of Italian bread
1 garlic clove
2 parsley sprigs, chopped
3/4 cup red wine
1 tbsp. catsup
2 cans minced clams with liquid (7 1/2 oz.)
1 cup clam juice
1/4 tsp. pepper
1/2 tsp. crumbled dried oregano

Heat 2 tbsps. oil in saucepan. Add bread
and brown on both sides. Remove bread
and add garlic to oil; cook for 2 or 3
minutes. Remove garlic. Add remaining
ingredients to oil and simmer for a few
minutes. Put a slice of bread in each
bowl. Pour in soup.

STEAMED CLAMS

Soft-shelled clams are best for steaming.
Allow 1 quart of clams per serving.

Scrub the shells thoroughly with a brush,
changing the water until there is no trace
of sand. Put in a deep kettle. Add 2
tbsps. water for each quart of clams.
Cover closely and cook over low heat until
the shells open a little (about 15 min.).
Do not overcook. Remove with a perforated
spoon to large soup plates. Serve with
individual dishes of melted margarine. If
you like, add a few drops of lemon juice
or vinegar to the margarine. If a small
quantity of boiling water is put into the
dishes, the melted margarine will float on
top and remain hot much longer. Strain
the broth left in the kettle into small
glasses and serve with clams.

CLAMS WITH RICE

1 medium onion, chopped
2 tbsps. margarine
2 tbsps. olive, sesame or peanut oil
2 cans (7 ozs. each) tiny whole clams
Water
1 1/2 cups canned tomatoes
1 cup uncooked rice
1/2 tsp. dried oregano leaves
Salt and pepper to taste

Saute onion in margarine and oil until
golden brown. Drain clams, saving the
liquid and adding enough water to make
1 1/2 cups. Combine all the ingredients.
Cover and simmer for about 25 minutes.

BAKED CRAB AND RICE CASSEROLE

1 medium-sized onion, thinly sliced
2 tbsps. salad oil
2 tbsps. margarine
1/2 cup catsup
1 tsp. Worcestershire sauce
Salt and pepper to taste
1 1/2 to 2 cups flaked fresh cooked or
   canned Dungeness crabmeat
2 cups cooked brown or white rice

Saute onion slowly in combined salad oil
and margarine until very tender. Add catsup and seasonings. Combine this sauce
with the crabmeat and rice. Turn into a
greased casserole. Cover and bake in 375-
degree oven until heated through, about
20 to 25 minutes.

NOTE: Substitute either cooked clams or
shrimp if crabmeat is not available.

CREOLE CRAB AND RICE CASSEROLE

2/3 cup uncooked rice
1 small onion, minced
1 small green pepper, chopped
2 tbsps. margarine
1 can tomatoes (19 ozs.)
1 tsp. seasoned salt
1/4 tsp. seasoned pepper
1 tsp. sugar
1/2 tsp. Worcestershire sauce
1 bay leaf
6 whole black peppers
1 can crabmeat (6 ozs.)

Cook and drain rice. Cook onion and
green pepper in margarine 2 or 3 minutes.
Add tomatoes and next 4 ingredients. Tie
whole spices in small piece of cheesecloth and add. Simmer uncovered, 10 min.
Discard cheesecloth with spices. Add
crabmeat, rice and salt and pepper to
taste. Put in 1 1/2 quart casserole.
Crumbled crackers may be spread over top.
Bake in 375-degree oven about 30 minutes.

CRAB GUMBO

2 pkgs. frozen okra, thawed
2 tbsps. margarine
2 tbsps. all-purpose flour
1 large onion, chopped
2 1/3 cups tomatoes (1 lb. 3-oz. can)
1 bay leaf, crushed
2 tbsps. chopped parsley
1/4 tsp. ground thyme
1/8 tsp. cayenne
1 garlic clove, minced
1 1/2 lbs. crabmeat
8 cups boiling water
1 tsp. salt
3 cups boiled rice

Slice okra into 1/2-inch pieces. Melt
margarine in bottom of heavy kettle.
Blend in flour, add okra, onion, tomatoes
with the juice, bay leaf, parsley, thyme,
cayenne, garlic, and crabmeat. Simmer
slowly for 10 minutes, stirring often to
keep okra from scorching. Add water and
salt. Simmer, covered, for 1 hour. Uncover and simmer until the consistency of
thick soup. Stir often. Put a scoop of
rice in each of 6 large soup bowls or
plates and ladle soup over it. Makes 6
servings.

BOILED LOBSTER

1 lobster, 1 to 2 lbs.
1/2 cup vinegar
1/2 tsp. powdered mustard
Juice of one lemon
1 tbsp. chopped celery
1 tbsp. chopped parsley
4 tbsps. oil
1 tbsp. water
Salt and pepper to taste

Boil the lobster in water to which salt
and vinegar have been added. Cook for
about 20 minutes or longer, depending on
the size of the lobster. Let cool. Remove lobster, clean and cut tail into
small pieces. Put into a deep bowl the
green and red eggs of the lobster, the
powdered mustard, lemon juice, parsley,
oil, tablespoon of water and salt and
pepper. Beat together until all ingredients are thoroughly mixed. Pour
this sauce over the lobster, adding a few
hearts of celery finely chopped, if
desired.

OYSTER AND SHRIMP JAMBALAYA

2 tbsps. olive or salad oil
1 pint oysters
2 onions, chopped
1 garlic clove, pressed
1 small green pepper, minced
1 lb. raw shrimps, shelled and deveined
1 cup uncooked rice
2 cups tomatoes (1-lb. can)
2 cups water
1 bay leaf
Pinch of ground thyme
1 tsp. salt
1/8 tsp. pepper
1 tsp. sugar
Minced parsley

Heat oil in large skillet. Add oysters
and cook over low heat until edges begin
to curl. Remove from pan; cool. Cook
onions, garlic, and green pepper in
skillet for 2 to 3 minutes. Add shrimps.
Cook until shrimps turn pink. Remove
from pan. Put rice in skillet; heat,
stirring constantly, until rice browns.
Add tomatoes, water, and seasonings.
Cover and simmer over low heat until
rice is tender and liquid has been absorbed. Add oysters and shrimps. Heat
through, stirring gently. Serve gar-
nished with minced parsley. Makes 6
servings.

BROILED OR SAUTEED OYSTERS

1 pint shelled oysters
2/3 cup cracker crumbs
1/2 tsp. salt
1/8 tsp. pepper
1/4 cup melted margarine
Toast

Drain oysters and pat dry on a paper towel. Mix cracker crumbs, salt and pepper. Dip oysters in melted margarine, then in crumb mixture. Broil on a greased broiling rack 2 inches from the heat, or saute in 2 tablespoons margarine. Turn once while cooking. Serve on toast.

SCALLOPED OYSTERS

2 cups oysters
Margarine for oiling pan
1 cup fine bread crumbs
1/2 cup coarse cracker crumbs
1/2 cup margarine
1 tsp. salt
1/4 tsp. pepper
1 cup oyster liquid

Drain and clean oysters. Oil baking dish and cover bottom with part of bread crumbs. Combine remaining bread crumbs with cracker crumbs, margarine, salt and pepper. Arrange oysters and crumb mixture in layers. Pour on oyster liquid. Bake 35 minutes in 400-degree oven.

PEPPER PAN ROAST

1/4 cup minced onion
1/4 cup minced green pepper
1 garlic clove, crushed
1 cup margarine
1 pint oysters

Cook onion, green pepper, and garlic in the margarine for 2 or 3 minutes. Remove garlic, add drained oysters, and cook until plump, a very few minutes. Serve with toast. Makes 2 generous servings.

PRAWNS WITH TOMATO SAUCE

2 lbs. prawns
Boiling water
1 tsp. salt
1 bay leaf
1 large onion, chopped
1/2 cup margarine
2 tbsps. olive, sesame or peanut oil
1 clove garlic, minced
1 6-oz. can tomato paste, diluted with
   1 can water
2 tbsps. white wine vinegar
1 tbsp. brown sugar
1/2 tsp. basil
Salt and pepper to taste

Cover prawns with boiling water. Add
salt and bay leaf and simmer for 12
minutes. Cool by rinsing in cold water,
peel and remove black veins. Saute
onion in margarine and oil until golden
brown. Add remaining ingredients and
simmer, uncovered, for 30 minutes. Add
prawns and heat. Serve on rice, if
desired.

BROILED SCALLOPS

Wash and dry 1 pound of scallops. Dip in
oil. Drain and season with pepper. Melt
4 tablespoons margarine. Add 1 1/2
tablespoons lemon juice and 1 1/4 tablespoons minced onion, chives, or leeks.
Stir and cook for 2 minutes. Place
scallops under broiler for 5 minutes.
Baste with above sauce. Turn and season
with salt. Serve hot.

SCALLOPS BROILED IN GARLIC SAUCE

1 lb. scallops
1/3 cup margarine
1 tbsp. chopped parsley
Salt and pepper
1 clove garlic, split
2 tsps. green onions
1 tsp. oregano

Brown the split garlic in margarine. Remove garlic, mix margarine with seasonings. Wash, drain scallops. Place in baking dish. Pour margarine mixture over them. Broil about 5 minutes, until scallops are done. Add lemon juice.

DEVILED SCALLOPS

1 lb. scallops
1 clove garlic, chopped
2 tbsps. melted margarine
2 tbsps. flour
1/2 tsp. dry mustard and celery salt
2 tsps. prepared horseradish
2 tbsps. chopped parsley
1 tbsp. lemon juice
Few grains pepper
1/2 cup buttered crumbs (margarine)
Paprika

Rinse scallops well to remove any sand. If large, slice them. Cook garlic in margarine until golden. Remove garlic and discard. Blend in flour and seasonings. Add scallops and cook from 4 to 5 minutes; stir constantly. Place in 4 greased individual shells or custard cups. Top each cup with 2 tablespoons crumbs. Garnish with paprika. Bake 20 minutes in 350-degree oven.

SKILLET SCALLOPS

2 lbs. scallops, fresh or frozen
  (shrimp or crab may also be used)
1 pkg. (7 oz.) frozen pea pods
1/4 cup margarine
2 tomatoes, cut into eighths
1/4 cup water
2 tbsps. cornstarch
1 tbsp. soy sauce
1/2 tsp. salt
1/8 tsp. pepper
3 cups hot cooked rice
Soy sauce

Thaw frozen shell fish and pea pods.
Rinse shell fish with cold water to remove any shell particles.

Cut scallops in half crosswise. Drain
pea pods. Melt margarine in a 10-inch
frying pan. Add scallops (or other shell
fish) and cook over low heat for 3 to 4
minutes, stirring frequently.

Add pea pods and tomatoes. Combine water,
cornstarch, soy sauce, salt and pepper.
Add to scallop mixture and cook until
thick, stirring constantly. Serve in a
rice ring with soy sauce. Yield: 6
servings.

SCALLOPS WITH RICE

1 large onion, chopped
1/4 cup margarine
2 lbs. sea scallops
1 cup uncooked rice
2 tbsps. olive, sesame or peanut oil
Water
1 1/2 tsps. salt
Parsley, chopped

Saute onion in margarine until golden.
Wash scallops and add to the onions. Simmer for 15 minutes, turning occasionally.
Brown rice in oil until golden and turn
into a 2-quart casserole. Drain liquid
from scallop mixture and add enough water
to make 2 1/2 cups. Add salt to the
liquid and pour over the rice. Cover and
bake in a 400-degree oven for 20 minutes.
Stir in scallop mixture and bake for 10
more minutes. Sprinkle with parsley.

BARBECUED SHRIMP

1 1/2 lbs. shrimp, washed and shelled
2 sprigs celery, chopped fine
1 tbsp. wine vinegar
1 tsp. salt
Dash of pepper
2 onions, chopped
1/3 cup salad oil
1 cup tomato sauce
1/2 cup water
1 clove garlic, minced
1/2 cup chopped parsley

Saute onion, celery and seasonings in oil,
stirring constantly until soft and golden.
Add shrimp, and stir over high flame until moisture is absorbed. Add vinegar,
then tomato sauce and water. Cook about
25 minutes. (A bay leaf may be added for
extra flavor).

BRAISED SHRIMP

2 lbs. shrimp
5 onions, sliced
1/2 cup oil
2 cups canned tomatoes
1 tsp. parsley, chopped

Cook shrimp with shells in water to cover
for 10 minutes or until tender. Drain,
reserving 1 cup of the broth. Shell and
devein shrimp. Saute onions in oil. Add
tomatoes, chopped parsley and 1 cup shrimp
broth and simmer for 20 minutes. Add
shrimp.

VARIATION: Increase broth to 2 cups and
bring to a boil. Add salt to taste and
add 1 cup rice. Cover and cook until
tender. Add shrimp.

BROILED SHRIMP

1 lb. shrimp
Olive or vegetable oil

Sauce:
    1 lemon, juiced
    1/3 cup oil
    1 tbsp. dill, finely chopped

Wash and clean shrimp. Brush with oil
and broil about 3 inches from heat for
5 minutes. Serve with sauce made by
combining lemon juice, oil and dill.

SHRIMP CREOLE

1 cup sliced onions
1/2 cup diced celery
1 clove garlic, minced
3 or 4 tbsps. oil
2 cups canned tomatoes
1 tbsp. vinegar
1 tbsp. flour
1 tsp. salt
1 tsp. sugar
2 to 3 tsp. chili powder
1 cup water
2 cups canned peas
2 cups cooked or canned shrimp

Cook first 3 ingredients until tender in oil in skillet over medium heat. Add combined flour, salt, sugar and chili powder mixed with 1/4 cup water. Add 3/4 cup water. Simmer, uncovered, for 15 minutes. Meanwhile, cook rice. Keep hot. When onion mixture has cooked 15 minutes, add tomatoes and rest of ingredients, except rice. Serve over rice or pack rice in a greased 1-quart mold. Unmold on plate. Place creole in center and around rice.

SHRIMP MARINARA

1 tbsp. salad oil
2 crushed garlic cloves
1 tbsp. chopped parsley
1 tbsp. sugar
1 tsp. salt
1/2 tsp. oregano
1/4 tsp. basil
1/8 tsp. pepper and cayenne
1 can (large) tomatoes
2 lbs. fresh or frozen shrimp (If using frozen shrimp, follow directions on package for cooking)
4 cups hot cooked rice

Heat oil, add garlic and saute. Add parsley, sugar, salt, oregano, basil, pepper and cayenne, and tomatoes (break up tomatoes). Bring this mixture to a boil, then simmer for 25 minutes. Leave skillet uncovered while simmering. Add shrimp to sauce and let simmer for 10 minutes, stirring. Place shrimp and sauce mixture on cooked rice and serve hot.

MARINATED SHRIMP WITH MUSHROOMS AND OLIVES

1 lb. fresh mushrooms, quartered
1 cup water
1/3 cup oil
2/3 cup vinegar
2 tbsps. lemon juice
2 cloves garlic, halved
1 1/4 tsps. salt
1/2 tsp. thyme leaves
1/2 tsp. peppercorns
1/8 tsp. nutmeg
2 bay leaves
3/4 cup small pimiento-stuffed olives
2 lbs. medium shrimp, cleaned and cooked

Combine mushrooms, water, oil, vinegar,
lemon juice and seasonings in saucepan.
Bring to a boil and cook, covered, 5
minutes.

Pour into a bowl; add olives and shrimp
and cool. Cover and chill 6 to 8 hours
or overnight before serving. Yield: 6
to 8 servings.

PARSLEY SHRIMP

1 lb. shrimp, cleaned and deveined
1 clove garlic, crushed
1/2 cup chopped parsley
4 tbsps. salad oil
4 or 5 tbsps. lemon juice
1/2 tsp. salt
Pepper to taste

Heat oil in skillet, add shrimp, salt,
pepper and crushed garlic, and saute for
5 minutes, stirring often. Add lemon
juice and chopped parsley; cook 5 min.,
adding water, if necessary.

G17

STEWED SHRIMP

2 lbs. large raw shrimps, shelled and deveined
3 tbsps. fresh lime juice
1 large sweet onion, very thinly sliced
2 medium-size tomatoes, peeled, seeded and
   diced
1 large garlic clove, minced or mashed
1 tbsp. finely snipped chives
1/2 tsp. salt
1/2 tsp. crumbled dried thyme
Dried crushed red pepper to taste (begin
   with 1/4 tsp.)
1/8 tsp. ground black pepper
1/4 cup margarine or salad oil
1/2 tsp. monosodium glutamate
1/2 tsp. curry powder

Sprinkle shrimp with lime juice and toss
to mix.

Add onion, tomato, garlic, chives, salt,
thyme, red pepper, and black pepper. Toss
gently to mix well.

Allow to marinate for 30 minutes at room
temperature or for 1 to 3 hours, covered
and chilled.

Just in time for serving, melt margarine
in a large frying pan. Stir in monosodium glutamate and curry powder. Add
shrimp with marinating mixture. Cover
and cook over medium heat just until
shrimps turn pink and onion is slightly
wilted, about 8 minutes. Turn shrimp
and stir gently once or twice. Serve
immediately over rice. Serves 6.

SHRIMP VEGETABLE SKILLET

1 lb. raw shrimp or 2 (5 oz.) cans
  shrimp
1/4 cup oil
1 large eggplant, peeled and cubed
1 medium onion, chopped
1 clove garlic, minced
1/4 cup minced parsley
1/4 cup water
1/2 tsp. salt
Dash pepper
4 slices dry bread, cubed

Cook shrimp in oil for 2 minutes. Remove shrimp. Add eggplant, onion, and
garlic, cooking until tender. Add next
4 ingredients plus shrimp. Cover and
simmer 15 minutes. Add bread cubes
(leave uncovered) and cook 5 minutes
longer. For variation, use scallops instead of shrimp.

PINEAPPLE AND SHRIMPS, CHINESE STYLE

1/4 cup firmly packed brown sugar
1 1/2 tbsps. cornstarch
1/2 tsp. salt
1/4 cup vinegar
1 tbsp. soy sauce
1/2 tsp. ground ginger
2 1/2 cups pineapple chunks (1 lb. 4 1/2-
  oz. can)
1 green pepper, cut into strips
1 medium onion, cut into rings
1 lb. shrimps, cleaned, shelled, cooked
Hot cooked rice.

Blend sugar, cornstarch, and salt in large
saucepan or skillet. Add vinegar, soy
sauce, ginger, and syrup from pineapple.
Cook, stirring constantly, until thickened.
Add pineapple, pepper, and onion; cook for
2 or 3 minutes. Add shrimps and bring to
boil, stirring. Serve on hot rice. Makes
4 to 6 servings.

GRILLED JUMBO SHRIMPS, VENETIAN STYLE

2 lbs. raw jumbo shrimps
1 garlic clove, crushed
Pepper to taste
Juice of 1 lime
1/4 cup olive or vegetable oil
Garlic sauce (see below)

With scissors or sharp knife, split each
shrimp shell on underside down to tail;
try not to cut meat. Put shrimps in bowl
with next 4 ingredients. Stir well to
coat shrimps. Cover and refrigerate for
at least 2 hours. Push onto skewers and
grill 6 inches from heat over low charcoal
fire, turning frequently. This takes
about 15 minutes. If grilling in broiler,
remove shells first. Serve with garlic
sauce.

Garlic Sauce:

Mix 1/2 cup melted margarine, 1 teaspoon
Worcestershire sauce, 1 tablespoon fresh
lemon juice, 1/4 teaspoon hot pepper
sauce, 1 mashed garlic clove, and salt
to taste. Serve in saucers as a dip for
shrimp.

SWEET-AND-SOUR SHRIMPS

2 lbs. cooked, shelled shrimps
2 cups pineapple chunks
2 tbsps. grated green or crystallized
  ginger root
1 green pepper, cut into long slivers
1/2 cup margarine or cooking oil
1 cup pineapple juice
1/4 cup sugar
1/2 cup vinegar
1 tbsp. soy sauce
2 1/2 tbsps. cornstarch
1/2 cup water

Split shrimps. Combine shrimps, pineapple chunks, ginger root, and green
pepper. Heat margarine and cook mixture
in it for 2 minutes. Add pineapple
juice, sugar, vinegar, and soy sauce.
Mix cornstarch with water to make a
paste. Stir into shrimp mixture and
cook over medium heat, stirring constantly, until thick and clear. Serve
with boiled rice.

SHRIMPS TERIYAKI

Split shrimps up the back with scissors
and pull out the sand veins. Marinate
in equal parts of pineapple juice, soy
sauce, and bland cooking oil. Thread
each shrimp onto a split bamboo or
wooden stick that has been soaked in
water. Broil or grill for 3 to 4
minutes on each side, and serve on the
sticks.

SPAGHETTI A LA KING CRAB

2 cans (7 1/2 ozs. each) Alaska king crab
   or 1 lb. frozen Alaska king crab
2 tbsps. oil
1/2 cup margarine
4 cloves garlic, minced
1 bunch green onions, sliced
2 medium tomatoes, diced, or 1 can
   tomato slices or wedges, drained and
   diced
1/2 cup chopped parsley
2 tbsps. lemon juice
1/2 tsp. Italian seasoning
1/2 tsp. salt
1 lb. spaghetti

Drain canned crab and slice. Or, defrost,
drain and slice frozen crab. Heat oil
and margarine. Add garlic and saute
gently.

Add crab, green onions, tomatoes, parsley,
lemon juice, Italian seasoning and salt.
Heat gently 8 to 10 minutes.

Meanwhile, cook spaghetti in boiling,
salted water just until tender. Drain
spaghetti. Toss with king crab sauce.
Yield: 6 servings.

SQUID PILAF

Starting from back of squid, cut through,
removing backbone. Then remove ink sack.
Wash squid well. Place squids with chopped
tentacles in deep saucepan, heat until
moisture is absorbed, 10 to 15 minutes.
Add 2 cups water, and bring to boiling
point. Stir in 1 cup rice and season to
taste. Cover, simmer 15 to 20 minutes,
or until rice is tender.

SAUTEED SQUID

Clean squids, remove ink sack and center bone. Wash well. Cut squid in half lengthwise. Melt 1/4 cup margarine in a large fry pan. Place squid and tentacles in pan. Saute until squid curls up and flesh turns white. As margarine and water are absorbed, add more margarine until all squid are sauteed.

NOTE: This is excellent served on the side of a dish of rice with stewed tomatoes on the rice.

STUFFED SQUID

12 squid (4 to 5 inches in length)
1 cup chopped onions
2 tbsps. chopped parsley
1/2 cup oil
1/2 cup rice, boiled and strained
2 tbsps. pignolias
2 tbsps. tomato paste
2 tbsps. chopped mint
Salt and pepper

Wash squid thoroughly, remove heads, bones and ink sacks. Cut the fins, leaving only the whole bag, and pulling out the black skin. Wash well and sprinkle with a little salt. Simmer onions and parsley and mint in saucepan with oil until onion is golden brown. Add rice, pignolias, tomato paste and salt and pepper to taste. Cook together a few minutes to blend flavors and set aside to cool. Stuff each squid with a teaspoonful of above mixture and arrange side by side in baking pan. When all have been stuffed, pour on top sauce made of: 1 small glass wine, 3 to 4 tablespoons oil, 3 to 4 tablespoons water and salt and pepper. Bake in moderate oven for 1 hour.

SQUIDS IN WINE

1 lb. squids
1 onion, chopped fine
Salt and pepper
1/3 cup salad oil
1/2 cup dry white wine
Chopped parsley

Clean squids, remove ink sack and center
bone. Wash well. Place squids with
chopped tentacles in deep saucepan, place
over high flame, and heat until moisture
is absorbed, about 10 to 15 minutes. Add
oil and chopped onion, and brown. Pour
wine over all, cover and simmer until
squids are tender, and season with salt
and pepper.

SHRIMP NOODLE SKILLET

2 tbsps. margarine
1/2 cup chopped green pepper
1 garlic clove, crushed
1/8 tsp. pepper
4 cups clam juice
About 4 cups (8 oz.) fine noodles
1 can (6 oz.) mushrooms
1/4 cup canned pimientos, chopped
2 cans (5 oz. each) shrimps, drained

Melt margarine in 10-inch skillet. Add
green pepper and garlic and cook over low
heat for 5 minutes. Add pepper and clam
juice and heat to boiling point. Gradually add noodles so that mixture continues to boil. Cook, uncovered, for 5
minutes, stirring occasionally. Add undrained mushrooms, pimientos, and shrimps.
Cook for 5 minutes longer, stirring occasionally, or until thoroughly heated.
Makes 4 to 6 servings.

V E G E T A B L E S

ARTICHOKES A LA POLITIKA

6 artichokes
3 lemons
4 tbsps. flour
12 small white onions, whole
1 1/2 cups olive or vegetable oil
Salt
Pinch of sugar
1/2 cup finely chopped onion
1/2 bunch finely chopped dill

Peel artichokes by cutting back top three
layers of leaves by hand to the breaking
point. Slice off one inch of tips and
small portion of stem. Scrape upper portion and stem of artichokes to remove all
traces of green. Remove purple choke
with spoon. Rub artichokes with lemon
and drop into bowl of cold water to which
has been added the juice of one lemon and
four tablespoons of flour. Brown chopped
onion in oil until soft, add whole white
onions, water to cover, juice of one
lemon, remaining oil, salt, and pinch of
sugar. Bring mixture to a boil and add
prepared artichokes and chopped dill.
Cook slowly about 30 minutes. Allow to
cool in sauce and serve cold.

ARTICHOKES AND LEMON SAUCE

Artichokes
Lemon juice
Salt

Sauce:
1/3 cup margarine
1 to 2 tbsps. lemon juice
Dash of cayenne

H5

Wash artichokes and trim stem to 1 inch.
Pull off tough outer leaves. Snip tips
from remaining leaves.

Stand artichokes in one inch boiling
water. Add 1 1/2 teaspoons lemon juice
for each artichoke. Sprinkle 1/4 teaspoon salt on each. Cover tightly and
boil 30 to 45 minutes until tender. Stem
can be pierced easily with fork when done.
Turn artichokes upside down immediately
to drain.

Serve with lemon sauce. Heat margarine
until browned. Stir in lemon juice and
add a dash of cayenne. Makes 1/2 cup
sauce.

SAVORY GREEN BEANS

2 tbsps. margarine
1 medium onion, minced
1 clove garlic, split
1 pkg. frozen green beans, thawed just
    enough to break up
1 tsp. salt
1/8 to 1/4 tsp. pepper
1/2 tsp. sugar
2 medium tomatoes, chopped, peeled or
    2 canned tomatoes

In margarine in large skillet, saute onion
and garlic until golden; discard garlic.
Add beans, salt, pepper, sugar and tomatoes. Cover and simmer 20 to 25 minutes,
or until beans are tender. Makes 4
servings.

STEWED GREEN BEANS WITH TOMATOES

1 garlic clove, minced
1 cup thinly sliced onion
2/3 cup chopped green pepper
2/3 cup diced celery
2 tbsps. margarine
2 cups chopped fresh tomatoes
2 cups cut fresh or canned green beans
1/2 cup chopped parsley
Salt and pepper

Saute garlic, onion, green pepper, and celery in margarine in heavy skillet for about 3 minutes. Add tomatoes, beans, and parsley. Cover and cook for 15 minutes, or until beans are tender or until canned beans are heated through. Season to taste. Makes 4 servings.

BRAISED STRING BEANS

1 large onion, chopped
1 small clove garlic, minced
3/4 cup olive or vegetable oil
1/2 can tomato sauce
Water
1/2 fresh tomato, peeled and chopped
1 lb. string beans
Parsley or fresh mint, chopped
Salt and pepper

Saute onion and garlic in oil until soft. Add tomato sauce and fresh tomato and simmer until sauce is slightly thickened. Add string beans and seasonings and enough water to cover. Cover and cook until beans are tender. Serves 4 to 6.

H7

FRESH BEETS IN ORANGE SAUCE

2 tbsps. grated orange rind
2 tbsps. fresh lemon juice
1 tbsp. fresh orange juice
1/4 tsp. salt
Pinch of pepper
1/8 tsp. ground nutmeg
1/4 cup margarine
4 cups sliced, peeled, cooked, fresh
    beets

Combine orange rind, lemon juice, orange
juice, salt, pepper and nutmeg in top of
double boiler. Add margarine and beets.
Heat well.

HONEYED BEETS

3 cups cooked beets, diced
2 tbsps. margarine
1 tbsp. grated orange rind
1/4 cup fresh orange juice
1/2 cup honey
1/2 tsp. salt
1/2 tsp. pepper

Place beets in heavy saucepan. Add all
other ingredients. Cook over low heat,
stirring constantly, until liquid has
evaporated and honey forms a glaze over
beets. Do not brown. Makes 4 servings.

RAISIN-SAUCED BEETS

1 1-lb. can (2 cups) sliced beets
1/3 cup light or dark raisins
1/4 cup sugar
1 tsp. cornstarch
3 tbsps. lemon juice
2 tbsps. margarine

Drain beets, reserving 1/3 cup liquid.
In medium saucepan, combine reserved beet
liquid and raisins. Cover; simmer until
raisins are plumped, about 5 minutes.
Combine sugar and cornstarch; stir into
raisins in pan. Add lemon juice and margarine; cook and stir over medium heat
until slightly thickened. Stir in beets
and simmer until mixture is heated through,
about 5 minutes. If desired, garnish
with a twist of lemon. Makes 4 servings.

BROCCOLI, CAULIFLOWER AND ARTICHOKE MEDLEY

1 pkg. frozen broccoli spears
1 pkg. frozen cauliflower
1 pkg. frozen or canned artichoke hearts
1 tbsp. finely chopped onion
1/4 cup margarine
1/8 tsp. salt
1/8 tsp. paprika
4 tsps. lemon juice
Diced pimiento

1. Cook broccoli spears, cauliflower and
   artichoke hearts separately, according to package directions. If using
   canned artichokes, heat. Keep vegetables hot.

2. Saute onion in margarine. Remove
   from heat. Stir in salt, paprika and
   lemon juice.

3. Arrange vegetables separately on dish.
   Drizzle lemon sauce over all.
   Sprinkle artichoke hearts with
   pimiento.

CABBAGE PLATE

3 cups coarsely chopped cabbage
2 cups sliced carrots
1 cup chopped celery
1 cup chopped onion
1 tbsp. sugar
1 1/2 tsps. salt
1/4 cup salad oil
1/2 cup hot water

Combine vegetables; add sugar, salt, oil and mix. Add water; cook until just tender, 10 to 15 minutes. Makes 8 servings.

HOT CABBAGE SLAW

6 cups shredded cabbage
1 1/2 tbsps. granulated sugar
1 tbsp. margarine
1/4 cup vinegar
1/4 cup water
1/8 tsp. paprika
Salt and pepper to taste

Shred cabbage fine and cook uncovered in boiling, salted water until tender--about 20 minutes. Drain and keep hot in serving dish. Melt margarine in top of a double boiler; add vinegar, sugar, paprika, salt and water and cook until hot. Remove from heat and pour over hot cabbage.

CAULIFLOWER PICKLE

1 medium head cauliflower
Boiling water
1 cup vegetable oil
2 tsps. grated ginger
1 clove garlic, crushed
1 tsp. ground coriander
1 tsp. crushed mustard seeds
1 tsp. crushed red pepper
1/4 tsp. turmeric
2 tbsps. cider vinegar
1 tbsp. brown sugar
1 tbsp. salt

Wash cauliflower and break into even-sized flowerets. Bring to a boil, drain and cool. Put into a jar or glass bowl. Combine remaining ingredients, pour over cauliflower and mix thoroughly. Cover and let stand at room temperature for 4 or 5 days. Makes about 5 1/2 cups.

CAULIFLOWER SAUTE WITH LEMON

1 cauliflower, medium-size
Olive or vegetable oil
Salt and pepper
Fresh lemon juice

Wash cauliflower and soak it in salted cold water for 1 hour. Drain, cut into flowerets. Cover with fresh, cold, salted water and cook slightly. The flowerets should be quite firm. Heat oil in a large skillet and add the drained flowerets. Saute them quickly, turning to brown on all sides. Remove to a hot serving dish and season to taste with salt and pepper; add lemon juice.

VARIATION: Serve cold, dressed with lemon juice, sesame seed oil, salt and pepper.

CHICK PEAS (GARBANZOS)

Take 1 cup raw chick peas (garbanzos), soak overnight, then boil until well-cooked. Smash thoroughly in a deep dish; add same quantity of sesame tahini and ingredients as used for broiled eggplant below.

BROILED EGGPLANT

Broil one medium-sized eggplant. Remove skin, smash into a thorough pulp. Add 3 tablespoons sesame tahini, lemon and salt to taste, mixing thoroughly. Place in flat dish adding olive oil and chopped parsley on top. A little garlic can be used if desired.

FRIED EGGPLANT

Either long or round eggplants may be used. Cut in thick slices without peeling. Sprinkle with salt and dip in flour. Fry in hot oil until golden brown and crispy. Delicious with skordalia (garlic sauce). (See recipes for sauces).

VARIATION: Zucchini squash may be scraped, sliced and fried in the same manner.

EGGPLANT ISTANBUL

1/2 cup salad oil
1 eggplant, peeled and cubed
1 onion, chopped fine
2 cloves garlic, crushed
2 tomatoes, peeled and cut in eighths
1 can tomato paste
Juice of 1 lemon
Salt to taste

Put oil, eggplant, and onion in saucepan
and cook for 10 minutes. Add garlic,
tomatoes, tomato paste, and juice of one
lemon. Simmer for 15 minutes. Add salt
to taste. Serve with lemon wedges or
spoon over fluffy steamed rice and add
an extra squeeze of lemon juice.
Serves: 6.

EGGPLANT AND OKRA

1 eggplant, peeled and cubed
1 onion, sliced
3 tomatoes, quartered
12 okra pods, sliced
Salt and pepper

Put all ingredients in a saucepan. Cover
and cook slowly for 30 minutes. Sprinkle
with finely chopped parsley, if desired.

SCALLOPED EGGPLANT

1 eggplant, cut in 1/2-inch cubes
Boiling water or 1/2 cup dry white
   wine
2 tbsps. margarine
1/2 onion, chopped fine
Buttered crumbs (margarine)
1 tbsp. parsley, finely chopped

Cover eggplant with boiling water or
wine. Cook until just tender and drain.
Cook onion in margarine until yellow.
Add the eggplant and parsley. Put in a
greased dish. Cover with buttered
crumbs. Bake in 375-degree oven until
the crumbs are brown. Serves: 4 to 6.

EGGPLANT WITH SESAME

1 large eggplant
3 tbsps. sesame paste (tahini*)
Juice of 2 medium lemons
1 garlic clove, crushed
Salt to taste
Olive or other oil
Parsley and/or pomegranate seeds

Broil eggplant over coals until skin is
charred and pulp soft, or roast in oven;
the former gives a desired smoky taste.
Peel and mash pulp until smooth. Add 1
tablespoon water to sesame and stir. Add
lemon juice, garlic, and salt to taste,
and combine with eggplant. Chill thoroughly and spread on flat plate. Make slight
depression in center and fill with oil.
Decorate with parsley or fresh pomegranate seeds, or both.

*Sesame paste is available in food stores
specializing in Near Eastern products and
in health food stores.

EGGPLANT-ZUCCHINI MEDLEY

1 eggplant, peeled and cubed
1 zucchini or summer squash, cubed
6 tomatoes, peeled and cut in pieces
1/4 cup oil
1 onion, chopped fine
1 clove garlic, crushed
1 tbsp. chopped parsley
1 bay leaf
Salt and pepper

Cook eggplant and squash in boiling water
for 10 minutes and drain. Put oil in
saucepan; add onion and cook until brown.
Add all vegetables and seasonings; cook
until tender. Season to taste. Place in
shallow baking dish; top with buttered
crumbs (margarine). Brown under broiler.
Serves: 6.

OKRA IN TOMATO SAUCE

2 lbs. okra
3/4 cup oil
3 onions, chopped
1 can tomato sauce
Juice of 1 1/2 lemons
Salt and pepper
Chopped parsley
1 cup water

Wash okra carefully, and trim the stems.
Dip stem ends in salt; place in deep
bowl. Sprinkle with lemon juice; let
stand 30 min., or overnight in refrigerator. Saute onions lightly in oil. Add
tomato sauce, water, parsley, and dash of
pepper. Bring to a boil. Add okra, reduce heat, and simmer until okra is
cooked and sauce has thickened. Additional water may be added to prevent
scorching.

NOTE: To use frozen okra, thaw 1 package
frozen okra in cold water. Rinse well
and drain. Cook 2 sliced onions in 4
tbsps. oil until soft. Add 2 tbsps.
chopped parsley, 1/2 cup tomato sauce,
3/4 tsp. salt and 1 cup water. Bring to
a boil and add okra. Reduce heat and
simmer for 15 to 20 min., or until okra
is cooked and sauce has thickened.

ONIONS EN CASSEROLE

3 cups small, white onions
1/2 cup catsup
1/3 cup honey
1 tbsp. margarine

Parboil peeled onions in boiling, salted
water about 5 minutes. Drain. Place in
1-quart casserole. Cover with catsup and
honey. Dot with margarine. Cover and
bake in 375-degree oven until tender--
about 45 minutes. Uncover last 15 minutes
of baking. Medium onions may also be used.

GLAZED ONIONS

12 to 15 small white onions
5 tbsps. margarine
2 tbsps. sugar

Peel onions; add water to cover and cook
until tender; drain. Melt margarine and
sugar in heavy skillet; add onions and
cook over low heat 15 minutes or until
golden.

STUFFED ONIONS

6 large, mild onions
1 cup cooked rice
1 can mushrooms, drained (4 oz.)
1/2 cup chopped, blanched almonds
2 tbsps. margarine

Cook onions in boiling, salted water for
30 minutes. Drain and cool. Remove center of onions. Combine rice, mushrooms,
almonds and margarine. Stuff the onions
with this mixture; cover and bake in
350-degree oven for 30 minutes.

SAUTEED PARSNIPS

1 dozen medium-size parsnips
4 tbsps. margarine
Salt and pepper
Parsley to garnish

Scrape or peel parsnips and boil until
tender. Drain and cool. When ready to
saute, melt 2 to 3 tablespoons margarine
in large heavy frying pan. Do not over-
heat. Pan should not smoke. Cut parsnips in long, thin slices about 1/3 of an
inch thick. Season each slice with salt
and pepper. Saute in hot margarine until
slices are flecked with golden brown.
Garnish warmed serving dish with parsley
on which slices are arranged. Dot slices
with remaining margarine. Serve hot.

SAVORY PEAS

1/2 cup sliced green onions
2 tbsps. margarine
1 1/2 cups shelled fresh peas (1 1/2 lbs.)
1/2 tsp. sugar
1/4 tsp. powdered savory
1/4 tsp. dried basil
1 tbsp. snipped parsley
1/2 cup water
1 tsp. salt
1/8 tsp. pepper

Saute green onions in margarine for 5
minutes, or until tender. Add peas,
sugar, herbs, water, salt, and pepper.
Cook covered, over low heat for 10
minutes, or until peas are tender.

PEAS WITH MUSHROOMS AND ONIONS

1 1/2 tbsps. margarine
2 tbsps. water
1/2 cup thinly sliced mushrooms
1 1/2 cups shelled fresh peas or 1 pkg.
  frozen peas (10 ozs.)
1 small onion, thinly sliced
1/2 tsp. salt

Melt margarine in saucepan. Add remaining ingredients. Cover pan tightly, and
cook until peas are tender. Shake pan
occasionally. Makes 4 servings.

POTATO-AND-ONION CAKE

4 medium potatoes
Margarine
3 onions, chopped
Salt and pepper to taste
Fine dry bread crumbs

Peel potatoes and slice very thin. Melt
margarine in heavy skillet. When hot,
add alternate layers of potatoes, onions,
and seasonings. Sprinkle top layer with
crumbs. Cook slowly until well-browned
on bottom and nearly done. Turn out on
flat plate. Add more margarine to skillet
and slide potatoes back into pan, brown
side up. Cook until browned. Turn out
to serve.

POTATO CUTLETS

1 big potato per person
Self-rising flour--flour with a little
  baking powder added
Salt and pepper
Finely minced onion

Grate the raw potatoes with a medium
grater. Add flour, salt, pepper, and
onion to make a "pap". Mix well. With
a tablespoon, put into hot oil and fry
until golden brown on both sides. May
be served with a green salad and gerkins.

BRAISED POTATOES

2 to 3 onions, finely chopped
1/2 cup olive or salad oil
6 to 8 medium potatoes, peeled and
   sliced
2 tbsps. tomato paste
Salt and pepper
Water to cover

Saute onions in oil until golden brown.
Add potatoes, tomato paste, salt and
pepper, and enough water to cover. Cover
casserole, bring liquid to a boil and
simmer for about 30 minutes or until
potatoes are cooked. Cool a little before serving. Serves 6.

SPINACH PIES

Dough:
2 to 3 lbs. flour
1/2 cup oil
2 cakes yeast
1 tbsp. salt
About 3 cups lukewarm water

Mix ingredients to knead with water.
Cover for about 1 1/2 hours. When risen,
cut into small pieces (about 36) and roll
into balls. Cover and let rise 30 more
minutes. Flatten to thinness of pie
dough and add filling, folding into tri-
angular shape.

Filling:
2 to 3 lbs. spinach
3 onions chopped fine
1 cup ground walnuts and/or pignolia nuts
Pepper and allspice to taste
1 cup corn oil
Salt
Juice of 3 lemons

Wash spinach thoroughly and cut into small
pieces. Sprinkle with salt and squeeze
until all water is removed. (Defrost frozen chopped spinach and squeeze and drain
dry). Add rest of ingredients and mix
well. Bake at 350 degrees for 20 minutes.

APPLE-FILLED SQUASH

2 acorn squash
Margarine
Brown sugar
2 1/2 cups applesauce
Jelly (if desired)

Wash squash; cut in half and remove seeds.
Bake cut side down in 350-degree oven for
35 minutes; turn and continue baking for
25 minutes more. Then brush inside with
margarine and sprinkle with brown sugar.
Heat applesauce and spoon into squash.
Garnish with jelly, if desired.

GLAZED SQUASH CROWNS

2 acorn squash
Salt
1/4 cup margarine
2/3 cup brown sugar

Cut squash in rings; remove seeds. Season.
Bake in covered 2-quart dish in 350-degree
oven for 30 to 40 minutes. Cream margarine
with brown sugar. Sprinkle over squash.
Bake uncovered until glazed.

SCALLOPED HUBBARD SQUASH

1 onion, chopped
1 green pepper, chopped
3 tbsps. margarine
3 1/2 cups mashed, cooked Hubbard squash
   or 2 boxes thawed frozen squash (12 oz.
   each)
Salt and pepper
1/2 cup crushed corn flakes

Cook onion and green pepper in margarine
until tender. Add squash and season with
salt and pepper to taste. Put in shallow
baking dish and sprinkle with crumbs.
Bake in 400-degree oven for about 30 min.

SQUASH MANDARIN

2 lbs. summer squash
Salt to taste
1 tbsp. margarine
1 can mandarin oranges (8 ozs.)
2 tsps. light brown sugar
1/4 tsp. ground nutmeg
1/4 cup toasted slivered almonds

Wash squash. Cut, unpeeled, into crosswise slices. Cook in small amount of
boiling water until just tender; drain
and add margarine. Keep warm. Pour
syrup from oranges into saucepan, add
sugar, and bring to boil. Add nutmeg
and orange segments. Pour over squash
and sprinkle with nuts.

YELLOW SQUASH WITH LEMON DRESSING

2 lbs. yellow squash
1/3 cup salad oil
Oregano
1 tsp. salt
1/3 cup lemon juice

Scrape skin of squash and wash well. Split
each squash in half, then cut in 1-inch
slices. (If squash is large, cut lengthwise in fourths before slicing). Cover
with water, add salt, and cook until tender. Drain well. With fork, beat oil and
lemon juice until thick. Pour over squash
and sprinkle with oregano. Salt and pepper
to taste. Serve warm or cold.

SQUASH PLAKI

2 lbs. yellow squash
2 onions, thinly sliced
3 fresh tomatoes, sliced or 1 can whole
  tomatoes
1/2 cup chopped parsley
Salt and pepper
5 tbsps. oil

Scrape outer skin of squash, wash, and cut
in small pieces. Combine all ingredients
in baking pan and bake in 375-degree oven
until vegetables are soft.

SWEET-POTATO APPLE CRISP

2 1/2 cups apple slices (1 lb. 4 oz.-can)
2 cups very thin slices of peeled sweet
  potatoes
1 tsp. ground cinnamon
1/2 tsp. salt
2 tbsps. fresh lemon juice
1/2 cup unsifted all-purpose flour
1/2 cup firmly packed brown sugar
1/3 cup margarine

H22

Drain apples; add enough water to juice to
make 6 tbsps. liquid. Alternate layers of
apples and potatoes in shallow 1 1/2-quart
baking dish. Sprinkle with mixed cinnamon
and salt. Mix liquid and lemon juice; pour
over first mixture. Combine flour and
sugar; cut in margarine. Sprinkle over top.
Cover and bake in 350-degree oven for 30
minutes. Uncover and bake for 15 minutes
longer. Makes 6 servings.

SCALLOPED SWEET POTATOES AND CHESTNUTS

4 medium sweet potatoes
1 lb. chestnuts
Salt to taste
3/4 cup firmly packed brown sugar
1/4 cup hot water
1/4 cup margarine

Cook, peel and halve sweet potatoes. Cover
chestnuts with boiling water. Simmer,
covered, for about 20 minutes. Rinse in
cold water and remove shells and skins.
Keep nuts in large pieces and arrange with
sweet potatoes in shallow baking dish.
Sprinkle with salt. Bring to boil brown
sugar and hot water. Add margarine. Pour
over ingredients in casserole. Bake, uncovered, in 350-degree oven for 30 minutes.

SCALLOPED SWEET POTATOES AND CRANBERRIES

6 sweet potatoes
1 1/2 cups whole-berry cranberry sauce
3/4 cup water
1/2 cup firmly packed brown sugar
3/4 tsp. grated orange rind
3/4 tsp. ground cinnamon
1 1/2 tbsps. margarine

Cook and drain potatoes. Peel; cut into
halves lengthwise and arrange in baking
dish. In saucepan mix remaining ingredients except margarine. Simmer, uncovered for 5 minutes. Add margarine,
stir until margarine is melted. Pour over
potatoes and bake, uncovered, in 350-
degree oven for 20 minutes, or until
glazed and hot.

TAHINI SPREAD

Mix equal parts of tahini and honey,
syrup or molasses. Spread on bread.

HOT SPICED WHOLE TOMATOES

6 firm ripe tomatoes
1/4 cup margarine
1 onion, minced
1/4 cup firmly packed light brown sugar
1/2 tsp. ground ginger
1/4 tsp. ground allspice
1/4 tsp. ground cinnamon
1/2 tsp. salt
2 tbsps. cider vinegar

Peel tomatoes, but do not remove stem
ends. Melt margarine in skillet; add
onion and saute for 2 to 3 minutes. Add
sugar, spices and salt; mix well. Arrange
tomatoes, stem end down, in the sugar mixture. Cover and simmer for 5 minutes over
low heat. Uncover and add vinegar. Cook,
covered, over very low heat for 45 minutes,
basting occasionally with sauce. Do not
stir. Carefully remove to serve. Makes
6 servings.

SAVORY TOMATOES, BEANS, AND SQUASH

1 large onion, sliced
1 garlic clove, minced
1/4 cup minced parsley
2 tsps. salt
1/4 tsp. pepper
1/4 tsp. ground thyme
1/4 tsp. ground sage
2 tbsps. cooking oil
1 lb. green or wax beans, cut
3 large tomatoes, diced
2 cups diced yellow squash

Cook onion, garlic, parsley and seasonings
in oil in large skillet for about 3
minutes. Add remaining ingredients. Add
water to half the depth of mixture. Cover
and simmer for 20 minutes, or until beans
are tender.

TOMATOES STUFFED WITH MACARONI

4 large ripe tomatoes
1 onion, chopped
1/2 green pepper, chopped
1/4 cup chopped celery
2 tbsps. margarine
2 cups cooked macaroni
Salt and pepper to taste

Cut a thin slice from stem end of unpeeled
tomatoes. Scoop out centers, leaving outer
wall. Reserve centers. Cook onion, green
pepper and celery in margarine for about
5 minutes. Add tomato centers, and cook
for 10 minutes. Combine with macaroni.
Season to taste with salt and pepper. Fill
tomatoes. Bake in 375-degree oven for about
30 minutes.

BAKED VEGETABLE DINNER

1 lb. potatoes
1 lb. okra
1 lb. squash
1/4 cup parsley
Salt and pepper
1 lb. tomatoes, fresh or canned
1 lb. onions
1 cup oil
1 sprig dill

Peel potatoes and prepare vegetables.
Slice potatoes, onions, squash and okra.
Arrange vegetables in layers. Sprinkle
dill and parsley between layers--also
salt, pepper and oil. Add a little water
and bake in 350-degree oven about 1 hour
or until done.

ZUCCHINI IN TOMATO SAUCE

2 tbsps. olive or other oil
1 garlic clove, finely chopped
7 cups Italian plum tomatoes (two 1 lb.
  13-oz. can)
1 tsp. salt
1 tsp. sugar
1/2 tsp. pepper
3 tbsps. tomato paste
12 small zucchini, peeled
2 tbsps. chopped fresh basil

Heat the oil, add the garlic and cook for
3 minutes. Add the tomatoes and bring to
a boil. Lower the heat and simmer slowly
for 20 to 25 minutes, stirring occasionally. Add next 3 seasonings and tomato
paste and simmer for 10 more minutes. Add
the zucchini and cook until just pierce-
able with a fork, about 15 minutes. Stir
in the basil and cool. Serve cold.

A P P E N D I X

A P P E N D I X

DAYS OF FAST - AN OUTLINE

The days of Fast in the Orthodox Catholic Church are as follows:

1.) The Eve of the Feast of the Nativity of Our Lord: Dec. 24/Jan. 6.
2.) The Eve of the Feast of the Theophany (the Baptism of Christ):
    Jan. 5/18.
3.) The Feast of the Beheading of St. John the Baptist: Aug. 29/
    Sept. 11.
4.) The Feast of the Exaltation of the Venerable Cross: Sept. 14/27.
5.) All Wednesdays and Fridays throughout the year, with the exception
    of these "fast-free" weeks and days:

    a.) The Week that follows the Sunday of the Publican and the
        Pharisee.
    b.) Cheese Fare Week (the week after Meat Fare Sunday--
        during this week all foods except meat and meat products
        are permitted).
    c.) Paschal Week (the week after the Sunday of Pascha).
    d.) Pentecost Week (the week after the Sunday of Pentecost).
    e.) Christmas Season: Dec. 25/Jan. 7 through Jan. 4/17.

J2

f.) Pentecost Season: from the week that follows Thomas Sunday up to and including the week before Pentecost, oil and wine are permitted on all Wednesdays and Fridays.

g.) Apodosis of Pascha is fast-free.

h.) And also, throughout the year, on certain Saint's Days, olive oil and wine are permitted (see list at the end of this Appendix).

DAYS	THE HOLY CANONS SPECIFY THE FOLLOWING:	
	ABSTINENCE OF:	NO ABSTINENCE OF:
Dec. 24/Jan. 6 Jan. 5/18 Aug. 29/Sept. 11 Sept. 14/27	Meat & Meat Products Dairy Products Fish Olive Oil Wine	Shellfish Vegetables & Vegetable Products Fruit
All Wednesdays and Fridays (see exceptions above)	On these days of fast Orthodox Christians regulate both the amount of food they consume and the number of times per day they eat. In other words, No food should be eaten between meals and at meals only a small portion of food should be eaten. It is also often customary to eat only once a day.	

SEASONS OF FAST - AN OUTLINE

The seasons of Fast in the Orthodox Catholic Church are as follows:

1.) The Christmas Fast (Advent): Nov. 15/28 through
    Dec. 24/Jan 6.

2.) The Fast of the Holy Apostles (The Peter & Paul Fast):
    From sundown on All Saints Sunday through June 28/July 11.

3.) The Theotokos' Fast: Aug. 1/14 through Aug. 14/27.

4.) The Great Fast: From sundown on Cheese-Fare Sunday through
    Great & Holy Saturday.

THE CHRISTMAS FAST AND THE FAST OF THE HOLY APOSTLES - AN OUTLINE
                                                    (Below)

DAYS	THE HOLY CANONS SPECIFY THE FOLLOWING:	
Sunday Monday Tuesday Thursday Saturday	ABSTINENCE OF: Meat & Meat Products Dairy Products	NO ABSTINENCE OF: Fish Shellfish Vegetables & Vegetable Products Olive Oil Fruit
Wednesday Friday	Orthodox Christians maintain the same fast & abstinence on these days as they do on all Wednesdays, Fridays & other days of Fast (see outline on previous page).	

NOTE: During the Christmas Fast, from Dec. 13/26 to Dec. 24/Jan. 6 inclusive, the Fast becomes stricter, and olive oil and wine are permitted only on Saturdays and Sundays. Also, fish is not permitted on any day during this period.

THE THEOTOKOS' FAST — AN OUTLINE
(Aug. 1/14 - 14/27)

THE HOLY CANONS SPECIFY THE FOLLOWING:

DAYS	ABSTINENCE OF:	NO ABSTINENCE OF:
Monday Tuesday Wednesday Thursday Friday	Meat & Meat Products Dairy Products Fish Olive Oil Wine	Shellfish Vegetables & Vegetable Products Fruit

On these days during the Theotokos' Fast, Orthodox Christians regulate both the amount of food they consume and the number of times per day they eat. In other words, no food should be eaten between meals and at meals only a small portion of food should be eaten. Also, it is customary to eat only once during the day.

(Continued Below)

J6

Saturday Sunday	Oil and wine are permitted on these days, in addition to the foods permitted on weekdays.
The Feast of the Transfiguration of Christ (Aug. 6/19)	ABSTINENCE OF: Meat & Meat Products Dairy Products NO ABSTINENCE OF: Fish Shellfish Vegetables & Vegetable Products Fruit Olive Oil Wine

NOTE: If the Feast of the Dormition of the Theotokos should fall on a Wednesday or Friday, the same foods are permitted as those permitted for the Feast of the Holy Transfiguration.

FOR THE PERIOD OF THE TRIODION AND THE GREAT FAST

WEEKS OR DAYS	THE HOLY CANONS SPECIFY THE FOLLOWING:
For the Week that follows the Sunday of the Publican and the Pharisee	All foods are permitted throughout this week.
Meat Fare Week (the week that follows the Sunday of the Prodigal Son)	This is a normal week. On Wednesday and Friday of this week, shellfish, vegetables, vegetable products and fruits are permitted but not olive oil and wine. All foods are permitted on all the other days of this week.

(Continued Below)

	ABSTINENCE OF:	NO ABSTINENCE OF:
Cheese Fare Week (the week that follows Meat Fare Sunday	Meat & Meat Products	Dairy Products Fish Shellfish Vegetables & Vegetable Products Fruit Wine Olive Oil

(Continued Next Page)

WEEKS OR DAYS	THE HOLY CANONS SPECIFY THE FOLLOWING:	
FROM	ABSTINENCE OF:	NO ABSTINENCE OF:
Sundown on Cheese Fare Sunday to Pascha	Meat & Meat Products Dairy Products Fish Olive Oil Wine	Shellfish Fruit Vegetables & Vegetable Products

During this period Orthodox Christians regulate both the amount of food they consume and the number of times per day they eat. In other words, no food should be eaten between meals and at meal time only a small portion of food should be eaten.

(Continued Below)

	ABSTINENCE OF:	NO ABSTINENCE OF:
Saturdays* and Sundays throughout the Great Fast *(All but Great Saturday on which a strict fast is kept)	Meat & Meat Products Dairy Products Fish	Shellfish Vegetables & Vegetable Products Fruit Olive Oil Wine

On Saturdays* and Sundays during the Great Fast the quantity and the number of times food may be consumed is not restricted.

(Continued Next Page)

J11

WEEKS OR DAYS	THE HOLY CANONS SPECIFY THE FOLLOWING:	
	ABSTINENCE OF:	NO ABSTINENCE OF:
Feast of the Annunciation (Mar. 25/Apr. 7) and Palm Sunday	Meat & Meat Products Dairy Products	Shellfish Fish Olive Oil Wine Vegetables & Vegetable Products Fruit

Clarification:

Dairy Products: butter, eggs, milk, cheese, etc.
Shellfish: oysters, shrimp, scallops, clams, etc.
Fish: sardines, tuna, trout, bass, pike, etc.
Wine: (extended to include whiskey, beer, etc.)

The regulations for fasting have been taken from all the Holy Canons and Interpretations found in THE RUDDER (Pedalion) which contains all the Sacred and Divine Canons of the One Holy Catholic and Apostolic Church - The Orthodox Christian Church.

THE FEAST DAYS ON WHICH OIL AND WINE ARE PERMITTED

Sept. 1 – Beginning of the Ecclesiastical Year. St. Symeon the Stylite.
Sept. 6 – Miracle of Archangel Michael in Chonae.
Sept. 8 – Birth of the Theotokos. FISH is also permitted on this day.
Sept. 9 – Sts. Joachim and Anna.
Sept. 13 – Consecration of the Church of the Holy Sepulchre in Jerusalem. Prefestival of the Venerable Cross.

Sept. 20 – St. Eustace (Eustathius) the Great Martyr and his family.
Sept. 23 – Conception of the Holy Forerunner and Baptist, John.
Sept. 26 – St. John the Theologian and Evangelist.

Oct. 1 – Holy Protection.
Oct. 6 – Holy Apostle Thomas.
Oct. 18 – Holy Apostle Luke the Evangelist.
Oct. 23 – St. James, the Brother of God and first bishop of Jerusalem.
Oct. 26 – St. Demetrius the Myrrh-streaming.

Nov. 1 – Sts. Cosmas and Damian of Asia Minor, the Unmercenary Healers.
Nov. 8 – Synaxis of the Archangel Michael and of all the Bodiless Hosts.
Nov. 12 – St. John the Almsgiver, Patriarch of Alexandria.
Nov. 13 – St. John Chrysostom, Patriarch of Constantinople.
Nov. 14 – Holy Apostle Philip. FISH is also permitted on this day.
Nov. 16 – Holy Apostle Matthew the Evangelist.

(Continued Next Page)

J13

Nov. 21 - Entry of the Theotokos into the Temple. FISH is also permitted on this day.

Nov. 25 - St. Catherine the Great Martyr. Apodosis of the Feast of the Entry of the Theotokos.

Nov. 30 - Holy Apostle Andrew the First-called.

Dec. 4 - St. Barbara the Great Martyr. St. John of Damascus.

Dec. 5 - St. Sabbas the Sanctified.

Dec. 6 - St. Nicholas the Wonderworker, Bishop of Myra of Lycia.

Dec. 9 - Conception by St. Anna of the Holy Theotokos.

Dec. 12 - St. Spyridon the Wonderworker, Bishop of Trimython of Cyprus.

Dec. 13 - Sts. Eustratius, Auxentius, Eugene, Mardarius and Orestes at Sebaste. St. Lucy of Sicily.

Dec. 15 - St. Eleutherius the Bishop-Martyr.

Dec. 17 - Holy Prophet Daniel and the Three Children Ananias, Azarias and Mishael. St. Dionysius of Zante.

Dec. 20 - Prefestival of the Holy Nativity of Our Saviour. St. Ignatius the God-bearer.

Dec. 25 - Holy Nativity of Our Saviour. All foods permitted up to and including Jan. 4/17.

Jan. 6 - Holy Theophany. All foods permitted.

Jan. 7 - Synaxis of Holy Forerunner and Baptist, John. FISH is also permitted on this day.

(Continued Below)

J14

Jan. 11 - St. Theodosius the Great, the Cenobiarch.
Jan. 12 - St. Sabbas of Serbia (The Church of Serbia and Greece celebrate St. Sabbas on Jan. 14).

Jan. 14 - Apodosis of Holy Theophany.
Jan. 16 - Veneration of the Precious Chains of St. Peter the Apostle.
Jan. 17 - St. Anthony the Great.
Jan. 18 - Sts. Athanasius and Cyril, Patriarchs of Alexandria.
Jan. 20 - St. Euthymius the Great.
Jan. 22 - Holy Apostle Timothy. St. Anastasius the Persian.
Jan. 25 - St. Gregory the Theologian.
Jan. 27 - Translation of the Holy Relics of St. John Chrysostom.
Jan. 30 - Three Hierarchs: Basil the Great, Gregory the Theologian and John Chrysostom.

Feb. 2 - Meeting of Our Lord God and Saviour, Jesus Christ. FISH is also permitted on this day.

Feb. 8 - St. Theodore the Commander. Holy Prophet Zachary.
Feb. 10 - St. Charalampus the Great Martyr.
Feb. 11 - St. Blaise the Hieromartyr. St. Theodora the Empress.
Feb. 17 - St. Theodore the Tyro.
Feb. 24 - The First and Second Finding of the Venerable Head of St. John the Baptist.

(Continued Next Page)

Mar. 9 - Holy Forty Martyrs of Sebasteia.
Mar. 25 - Annunciation of the Theotokos. FISH is also permitted on this day.

Mar. 26 - Synaxis of the Archangel Gabriel.
Apr. 23 - St. George the Great Martyr.
Apr. 25 - Holy Apostle Mark the Evangelist.
Apr. 30 - Holy Apostle James, brother of St. John the Theologian.
May 2 - Translation of the Holy Relics of St. Athanasius the Great.
May 8 - St. John the Theologian and Evangelist. St. Arsenius the Great.

May 11 - Sts. Cyril and Methodius, Equal to the Apostles.
May 15 - St. Pachomius the Great. St. Achillius, Archbishop of Larissa.
May 21 - Sts. Constantine and Helen, Equals to the Apostles.
May 24 - St. Simeon of the Wondrous Mountain.
May 25 - Third Finding of the Venerable Head of St. John the Baptist.
June 8 - Translation of the Holy Relics of St. Theodore the Commander.
June 11 - Holy Apostles Bartholomew and Barnabas.
June 24 - Birth of the Holy Forerunner and Baptist, John. FISH is also permitted on this day.

June 29 - Holy Apostles Peter and Paul. FISH is also permitted on this day.

June 30 - Synaxis of the Holy Twelve Apostles.

(Continued Below)

J16

July	1	–	Sts. Cosmas and Damian of Rome, the Unmercenary Healers.
July	2	–	Deposition of the Holy Robe of the Theotokos.
July	8	–	Kazan Icon of the Mother of God. St. Procopius the Great Martyr.
July	15	–	St. Vladimir, Equal to the Apostles. St. Cyriacus and his mother, St. Julitta.
July	17	–	St. Marina the Great Martyr.
July	20	–	Holy Prophet Elias.
July	22	–	St. Mary Magdalene the Myrrh-bearer. St. Marcella the Virgin Martyr.
July	25	–	Repose of St. Anna, Mother of the Theotokos.
July	26	–	St. Hermolaus. St. Parasceva of Rome.
July	27	–	St. Panteleimon the Unmercenary Healer and Great Martyr.
Aug.	6	–	Holy Transfiguration of Our Lord. FISH is also permitted on this day.
Aug.	15	–	Dormition of the Holy Theotokos. FISH is also permitted on this day.
Aug.	31	–	Deposition of the Venerable Sash of the Theotokos.

In addition to the above, oil and wine are permitted also on those days on which a local Saint is celebrated, or on days on which the local parish church celebrates its patron saint.

FASTING REGULATIONS PREPARED FOR COOK BOOK BY FR. MICHAEL HENNING, BUFFALO, N.Y. AND EDITED BY HOLY TRANSFIGURATION MONASTERY.

INDEX

SEAFOOD (continued)
  Prawns W/Tomato Sauce, G11
  Sauteed Squid, G23
  Scalloped Oysters, G10
  Scallops Broiled in Garlic
    Sauce, G12
  Scallops with Rice, G13
  Shrimp Creole, G15
  Shrimp Marinara, G16
  Shrimp Noodle Skillet, G24
  Shrimp Teriyaki, G21
  Shrimp Vegetable Skillet, G19
  Skillet Scallops, G13
  Spaghetti A La King Crab, G22
  Squid Pilaf, G22
  Squid in Wine, G24
  Steamed Clams, G5
  Stewed Shrimp, G18
  Stuffed Squid, G23
  Sweet-and-Sour Shrimp, G21
SESAME
  Eggplant with Sesame (Tahini),
    H14
  Sesame Asparagus Salad, F4
  Sesame Candy, C17
Shepherd's Pie, Soybean, E22
Sherry Sauce, Mushroom, F16
Shortbread, Apricot, C20
SHRIMP
  Barbecued Shrimp, G14
  Braised Shrimp, G14
  Broiled Shrimp, G15
  Fruit and Shrimp Boat, F9
  Grilled Jumbo Shrimp, Venetian
    Style, G20
  Marinated Shrimp, G17
  Molded Beans, Shrimp and Rice,
    G3
  Oyster and Shrimp Jambalaya,
    G9
  Parsley Shrimp, G17
  Pineapple and Shrimp, Chinese
    Style, G19
  Prawns W/Tomato Sauce, G11
  Red Snapper Steaks with
    Shrimps, D15
  Shrimp Creole, G15
  Shrimp Marinade, F20
  Shrimp Marinara, G16
  Shrimp Noodle Skillet, G24
  Shrimp Teriyaki, G21
  Shrimp Vegetable Skillet, G19
  Stewed Shrimp, G18
  Sweet-and-Sour Shrimp, G21
Sicilian Fish, D9

Skillet Scallops, G13
Skordalia, F16
Sliced Tomato Salad, F12
Smelts, D17
SOLE
  Fillet of Sole in Italian
    Sauce, D18
  Fillet of Sole in Wine, D19
  Spinach Stuffed Fish Fillets,
    (Sole), D20
  Vegetable Stuffed Fish Rolls,
    (Sole), D19
SOUPS
  Bean Soup, E3
  Bouillabaisse, D3
  Clam Chowder, G3
  Clam Soup, Italian Style, G5
  Crab Gumbo, G7
  Fish Soup, D9
  Lentil Soup, E13
  Lentil Soup with Tomatoes, E13
  Minestrone Milanese, E16
  Potato Soup, E20
  Quick Bortsch, E4
  Vegetable Soup, E25
  Vegetable Stock, E26
Soybean Shepherd's Pie, E22
Soy Butter Sauce, F16
SPAGHETTI
  Clam Sauce with Spaghetti, E8
  Crab Sauce with Spaghetti, E7
  Lenten-Style Spaghetti, E22
  Spaghetti A La King Crab, G22
  Spaghetti W/Garbanzo Sauce, E23
  Spaghetti W/Zucchini Sauce, E24
  Tomato Sauce (Spaghetti), F18
Spanish Rice, E21
SPICED
  Hot Spiced Whole Tomatoes, H24
  Spiced Powdered Sugar, C33
  Spicy Currant Bars, C22
SPINACH
  Spinach Pies, H19
  Spinach Rice, E24
  Spinach Stuffed Fish Fillets,
    D20
Spread, Tahini, H24
SQUASH
  Apple-Filled Squash, H20
  Baked Vegetable Dinner, H26
  Glazed Squash Crowns, H20
  Savory Tomatoes, Beans and
    Squash, H25
  Scalloped Hubbard Squash, H21
  Squash Mandarin, H21

ORDER FORM

ST. NECTARIOS PRESS
10300 ASHWORTH AVENUE NORTH
SEATTLE, WASHINGTON 98133-9410

Please send ____copy/ies of A LENTEN COOKBOOK FOR ORTHODOX CHRISTIANS at $8.50 each.

POSTAGE AND HANDLING:

U.S. $2.00 - 1st copy; $0.50 each additional copy
Outside of U.S.: $2.50 - 1st copy; $0.85 ea. additional copy
Payment in U.S. funds, please.

____ Please send information on our second lenten cookbook, LENTEN FAVORITES FOR ORTHODOX CHRISTIANS, available Fall/Winter 1991.

____ Please send sample copy of our parish bulletin, THE ORTHO-DOX CHRISTIAN WITNESS

____ Please send a complete catalog of over 300 items. ($1.00 without an order).

____ Please send information on discounts for parishes and book-stores on bulk orders of St. Nectarios Press publications.

(Please print)

NAME_____

ADDRESS_____

CITY_____ PROV/ STATE_____

POSTAL/
ZIP CODE_____ COUNTRY_____

HOLY TRANSFIGURATION MONASTERY offers the largest selection of mounted icon prints in the Americas, as well as hand painted icons, incense, and books, tapes of Byzantine Chant in English and Greek, and articles for Orthodox worship. A fully illustrated catalog is available for $5.00 from:

HOLY TRANSFIGURATION MONASTERY
278 WARREN STREET
BROOKLINE, MASSACHUSETTS 02146
(617) 743-0608

* * * * * *

HOLY NATIVITY CONVENT provides hand-sewn vestments and robes, liturgical items, hand-dipped pure beeswax candles, greeting cards and other items. Write for information and catalog to:

HOLY NATIVITY CONVENT
70 CODMAN ROAD
BROOKLINE, MASSACHUSETTS 02146
(617) 566-0156

* * * * * *

OTHER BOOKSTORES

Books and other religious articles are available from:

ST. JOHN'S BOOKSTORE
12 Mt. Pleasant Street
Ipswich, Massachusetts 01938
(508) 356-0259

A wide selection of <u>Greek</u> <u>and</u> <u>English</u> books, medals, prayer ropes, etc. are available from:

ST. MARK OF EPHESUS BOOKSTORE
850 South Street
P. O. Box 129
Roslindale, Massachusetts 02131-0219
(617) 469-2380

and

ST. NEKTARIOS BOOKSTORE
28 Flintwood Court
Willowdale, Ontario M2J 3P2 CANADA
(416) 491-7889